I0142256

FIGHT LIKE A LADY

ANYBODY CAN BE A B*!#%

ROBYN E. MURPHY

Thank you for purchasing this book!

If you need help with anything, feel free to get in touch.

Sincerely, Robyn Murphy

www.lifeinHim.us

Fight Like A Lady

Copyright © 2014 by Robyn E. Murphy

Published by Life Publishing

ISBN: 978-0-578-17598-0

Cover concept by EyeSocial Marketing & design by The ThumbPrint Group

All rights reserved. No part of this publication may be reproduced, stored in a retrieval system, or transmitted in any form or by any means, electronic, mechanical, photocopying or otherwise, without the prior written permission from the author. Unless otherwise indicated, all scripture quotations are taken from the New King James Version® (NKJV). Copyright© 1982 by Thomas Nelson. Used by permission.

All rights reserved. Scripture quotations taken from the Amplified® Bible (AMP), Copyright © 1954, 1958, 1962, 1964, 1965, 1987 by The Lockman Foundation Used by permission. (www.lockman.org). All rights reserved.

Scripture quotations marked (MSG) are taken from THE MESSAGE. Copyright © by Eugene H. Peterson 1993, 1994, 1995, 1996, 2000, 2001, 2002. Used by permission of Tyndale House Publishers, Inc.

Scripture quotations marked (NLT) are taken from the Holy Bible, New Living Translation, copyright ©1996, 2004, 2007, 2013 by Tyndale House Foundation. Used by permission of Tyndale House Publishers, Inc., Carol Stream, Illinois 60188. All rights reserved.

Printed in USA

DEDICATION

This book is dedicated to my three beautiful children, Daven, Joel and Aryel. Each with their own unique strengths, I've watched them war against the struggle to be like everyone else when they knew deep down inside they were cut from a different cloth.

As they would say, "The struggle is real," but I've watched each of them arise and conquer from the greater strength and character of love within them. Daven, Joel and Aryel, you are truly strengthened with all power and might in your inner man. With raised eyebrows and all, you still believed in me. Thank you. I love you throughout eternity.

TABLE OF CONTENTS

ACKNOWLEDGEMENTS

This being my first book has been one an incredible journey. Writing a book is no small feat. So many have been such a help and inspiration to me along the way. I'd like to thank Alice Muradyan and Carlo & Angela Alce' for their encouragement and prayers in my pursuit of the vastness of God.

There have been those who've held this project in prayer, some who've donated and made contributions towards the project and there are those who made advance purchases; all of who I'd like to acknowledge and say, *"Thank you!"*

Isaac & Ann Logan

Daven Murphy

Joel Murphy

Aryel Murphy

Richard & Rosalind Downer

Naomi Smith & Anekah Smith

Ps. George Logan

Esther Houston

Gregory Breda

Debbie Plair

Scott & Kelly McClintock

Daniele Lecesne

Guia Gulden

Nannette Clegg

Bryon Durham

Azniv Adamian

Debra Bell

Jeanine Monti

Donyel Smith

Karen North

Donya Morgan

Titicia Michaels

INTRODUCTION

Life is always filled with so many up, down and arounds. Who hasn't been faced with the day in and day out of consistently wretched people. They don't just go away. They're cutting you off on the freeway, taking forever in the coffee line and they most definitely keep a ruckus going in the office at work. Wacked people are everywhere, how do you get away from them or do you just believe life is crazy and go ahead and join the chaos?

In Fight Like A Lady, you'll discover the life hacks of a great fight and how to never let them see you sweat. We all have to deal with difficult people more often than we'd like. As Steven Furtick of Elevation Church would say, "problems have patterns". There are patterns to the problem people in our lives. Once you know the patterns of a winning fight, problematic people are diffused and become no more than stepping stones that aid in building a better you.

In Fight Like A Lady, you'll discover the real you that's made for so much more than succumbing to some of the irksome issues in life. This book is empowerment for dominion over yourself and your circumstances. You'll no longer be subject to the upset of others but walk in strength and power that controls your own environment and circumstances. You'll love being you.

1 THE LIFE IN ME

IT'S ON!

I want to open with the story that was the catalyst for this book. Ok. So here's the situation. I met this woman through a mutual guy friend. We had a few brief encounters. This woman with her cute little accent was just flat out rude. Regardless of how we met, I really tried to be kind and polite, but I kept getting hit with snide remarks and cat-clawing comments from her. It wasn't the petty, rude comments that made me angry, it was the provoking, antagonistic spirit in which she was doing this and right from the start—I just met the girl! This babe went for the jugular straight away. Okay, lady! It's on! Throwback from the thug life kicked in. My street instincts flared up; incapacitate, eliminate. I fought to suppress the fury as I contemplated which would be the preferred weapon of war, the sword of my tongue or an old-fashioned knockdown drag out.

I was really taken aback by the whole situation. We just met; we hadn't had time to get to know each other to decide whether or not we even liked each other. She came in swinging.

Evidently I posed a threat to her plans and she was all over it, from hello.

What is a nice Christian woman to do? Smile sweetly, turn the other cheek and ignore her or shift gears and jump right in? I grew up in the hood; the old me says to give her a good beat down, shake the dust off and put my halo back on.

I definitely wrestled back and forth with this one a lot longer than I would like to admit. My thoughts were filled with *She doesn't know me ... she doesn't know what I could do to her ... she started it; I'll finish it.*

My quiet, reserved demeanor can mislead one to think I'm a pushover. I remember as a child, one of my babysitters used to say, "It's the quiet ones that you have to watch." I didn't like that statement very much because she was talking about me. Now I know what she was referring to. With the quiet ones, it is easy to presume they're harmless because they don't give you a heads up on what they're thinking, when they'll strike or what could even ignite them. You really don't know how they're "taking" the situation. The babysitter was blowing my cover.

This girl thought I was some sweet little church girl that she could boot out of the way and nab the guy. Well, it was never about the guy for me, it was the principle of the matter. You don't treat me like that and get away with it, especially not over a guy. Women fighting over a guy has always seemed foolish to me. Any guy who's not astute enough to make a definitive decision between two women is really not ready for a quality relationship. (Just a side note there.)

Every woman is valuable and is to be highly esteemed. We must first see ourselves that way before others will know our true worth. In that moment, I was struggling with a lower identity of myself that I valued. I valued my abilities to lacerate with my tongue or beat a person down mercilessly. I later learned that those skills had a hidden gift. Without knowing their purpose, they were being used against me and others. One of my favorite authors, Dr. Myles Munroe, wrote in his book, *In Pursuit of Purpose*, "Wherever purpose is unknown abuse is inevitable." I will expound on that in later chapters.

By His grace, God came into my life at an early age. Generally speaking, I am a very reserved, quiet person. Although it would take a lot for me to get angry, when I did, it was like the pin from a grenade was pulled and there was no recapping it. From an early childhood, I had a severe temper. It wasn't wild and reckless; it was calculating and deadly. I would get so filled with anger that it would completely block my inner hearing and seeing. It was pure rage. Rage shifted into a strategic, calculated mode of fury. When I lost control, I was completely consumed. Sanity did not resume until the rage was not only avenged but also satisfied. At times, I have gotten so filled with rage, I have scared myself because I truly did not know what I would or wouldn't do. Whatever I came up with seemed justifiable at the moment.

To give you a little insight into my inner fury, I very much identified with Sylvester Stallone's character in the movie "First Blood" from 1982. He played a Vietnam veteran named Rambo who was sorely mistreated by a small town cop. They pushed him so far that finally he had to avenge himself. I totally agreed with everything he did; he was trying his best to keep peace, but they would not let up. He systematically and militarily rigged and blew up the entire town. To me, it was totally worth taking the whole town down.

I had to ask God to completely heal me of this because the older I got the worse it became. I was becoming afraid of myself. I began to rationalize why it was justifiable and whatever I chose to do to vindicate myself would be ok because, surely, I would be forgiven and they would go to heaven, maybe. If they hadn't gotten right with God by that point, it wasn't my fault. – God has, since that time, taught me compassion.

Being a committed Christian for over twenty years and a leader at my church, I knew the responsible thing to do in this situation was to ask God how to deal with this flaming irritant. She was persistent with her cat clawing digs and I was doing my best to maintain a calm, unprovoked temperament. Outwardly, I chose to be unresponsive to her. Inwardly, I was a volcano, ready to irrupt. It had been decades since I had last "lost my temper" uncontrollably. I wasn't sure how long I could do this because deep down inside I really wanted to go off on her and ask for forgiveness later. I wanted to have a reason to give her a severe beat down. I was really afraid of her provoking me at the wrong time or in the wrong place. The b*!#% in her was provoking the thug in me. I wanted to go blow for blow.

THE STRUGGLE IS ONLY REAL WHEN YOU GIVE IT REALITY

The fight to keep from responding on her level was where the real struggle was. My supporting thought and reasoning was that I had nothing to prove to her. I did not have to prove how Christian I was. I'm saved by His grace and His works; nothing in and of myself. The good works that I do are a result of who I've become in walking with Him and allowing Him to be the greatest influence in my life. It's not good works that make me a Christian, so doing something bad does not make me less of a Christian... That's no excuse to do anything wrong; it's just to say I do good things because of who I've become through my relationship with Jesus, not because of the title or name that comes with the relationship. When we realize it's about who we actually are and not the label, life becomes a lot easier to live. Living up to a label is always illusive because it's forever subject to perspective.

This situation was causing me to struggle with who I had become and the person I had left behind. I valued who I was before and what I could do, so I didn't want to let go of it because I knew I was good at it. We never want to let go of things we believe ourselves to be good at. We identify with the greatness in it, even though it may have the ability to cost us advancement. Pride in who you were can keep you from becoming what you were meant to be.

All it was going to take was a really good zinger on her part and it would be over... I'd squash the whole thing. My thought was, *Christians aren't perfect, just forgiven...* I felt like whatever I came up with to take care of her antagonistic behavior would be forgiven. If I had to resort to the brass knuckles, I'd dust myself off, ask forgiveness and continue my Christian walk with a sweet smile of satisfaction on the inside. My girlfriends would rally behind me and say how right I was to do whatever I came up with because, of course, she started it. Yes, I was being provoked and antagonized, but to fight like a b*!#% requires no strength at all, just an excuse.

People are people. No matter what they say they believe in, they are still people. All of mankind is cut from the same cloth—God Himself. It is He Who made man in His image and after His likeness. What we do with who we perceive ourselves to be is what makes us who we are and what we become.

Most people either expect Christians to be perfect or think that we think we're perfect... That is a huge deception. We are not perfect, and perfection cannot be attained in fallen humanity. Kill the struggle, surrender to His perfection and pursue excellence. A surrendered life in Christ gives us access to perfection Himself, Jesus; to influence our lives in as much as we're willing to give to Him. I choose to walk with Him, Who is perfect. Excuses just empower us to remain the same as we were. I could choose the new strength that I knew I had in Him or let the excuses legitimize who I used to be. That which I valued the most would win out.

It was the inner excuses that were feeding the ego of my old identity, trying to keep it alive. It requires strength to let go of the familiar to the walk in the new. A man of great wisdom, Al Hollingsworth, teaches, "let the lesser die, that the greater may live."

What separates true Christianity from all other religions is that everything we've done wrong in our lives has been paid for. Everybody has sinned, missed the mark, done wrong... There is no one on the earth that is sinless, other than Jesus. Sin has to be paid for and no one has laid down their life to pay for anyone's sin but Jesus. There is no religion on the planet that has said that any bad thing/wrong thing that you have ever done in your life has been paid for on your behalf but Christianity. It is unjust to think that anyone can get away with murder, lying, stealing, etc. and there's no price to pay. That's flat out foolish. We rage at injustices and atrocities all over the nations. The point is simple; either we accept the price that Jesus paid for everything we've ever done wrong in our life or we have to pay for it ourselves. Everyone has an appointment with death, which they will not miss. God judges in righteousness. He decided the rules before anyone had breath to refute anything that He'd already said, done, written and put in motion.

I was in a challenging situation because I was trying to have both, consciously choosing to act like who I knew I was not and still grow in who I had become. I knew the heart of God would forgive me and love me through that moment, but whichever I chose to do is what I would fortify in my life.

I remember asking God what to do; like I didn't already know. I was really trying to find out how I could lash out and not only be forgiven but be justified in it, and have God on my side. I really wanted Him to back me on this. He spoke very clearly, "fight like a lady, anybody can be a b*!#%." (For all the super Christians out there, NO, I'm not saying He actually said the "B" word, He just gave the inference as I did in the title) It really took me by surprise because I wasn't expecting that answer. I was looking for some really creative insight on how to get my way and have Him back me. I wanted a really great and creatively divine strategy on how to whack her really good and get away with it (which a lot of Christians do if they're honest with themselves). My response to Him was, "Why do I always have to be the good Christian?" His response to me was, "Why do you want to act like a b*!#%?" I was really losing this conversation. He was showing me that there was nothing significant about acting like that. Anybody can be a "B". It does not require any strength at all, just anger and a bad attitude. It is actually a display of weakness.

A friend once told me a story about when he was being teased in high school for carrying his Bible around. He was told that Bibles were for wimps. He told the guy who was teasing him, "Since you're so strong then you carry it." Strength is displayed in knowing who you are, and not bowing to a lower level or attitude that is beneath you. God saw me better and greater than I saw myself. He always sees us better than we see ourselves because He knows what He's put in us that is yet to be discovered.

The reality of true Christianity is not based on how perfect God has now made you, but on how grand His grace is in the face of your deepest, darkest, dirtiest ugly self. There is nothing you can do that His grace and salvation have not paid for. It doesn't exist. While we were all the ugliest of ugly, He was relentless in His pursuit of us. My whole motive was wrong, but He was loving me anyway.

REALITY WE CAN LIVE WITH

Even though so many things around us have influenced the perception that we have of ourselves and who we think we are, He wants us to know there is a reflection of Himself in each one of us. It's our choice as to what image we will feed on and reflect to others. There is nothing so bad or so horrifically ugly for God to deal with that His love and His grace do not exceed.

When I asked God about how to deal with the situation, He kept telling me that who I am in Him is far greater and stronger than who I was before I knew Him. The skills that I'd learned in my walk with Him were far superior to those of brawn and brute force from my old identity.

The poking and prodding at me was about me being provoked to operate on a lower level of identity than that of who I had become. You can't walk with someone on a daily basis and they not rub off on you, it just doesn't happen. You act like your five closest friends that you spend the majority of your time with.

Religious people don't spend time with God; they spend time making theoretical assumptions about God.

You can know all the factual information on me, my height, weight, physical appearance, likes, dislikes, friends, associates, favorite color, favorite books, favorite meal, etc. but you don't know me—those are facts that are presumed to be true and revealing about me. To truly know who I am as a person, you have to spend time with me and get to know my heart and why I make the choices I make. Without truly hearing my heart from me personally, all anyone would have is a subjective presumptuous opinion of me.

It's very easy to think you know someone when you know information about them. Celebrities can attest to this. People think they know a particular celebrity because they are their biggest fan and they've soaked up everything published about them. That is information through the filter of someone else's words and perception in the media. This type of knowledge is very limited and somewhat biased.

Spending time with God, just enjoying His company by sitting and having a conversation and reading my Bible, I got to know things about Him and He began to show me things about myself. It's as simple as that. Getting to know God is not complicated. He did all of the hard work. He closed the gap. All we have to do is draw near to Him and He draws near to us. He is the greatest example to want to be like and act like. When you read the Bible for yourself and don't wait for someone to tell you what it says, you'll find out amazing things about Him and the depth of His love. His Word is alive. Let Him tell you about Himself.

Whenever you go to God about someone, He generally likes to deal with you. Not that you're always the one in the wrong, but you are the one who is inquiring of Him... It's your ear that He has in the moment; you made the inquiry of Him. So if He can get you to do what He says, whatever He tells you will always take care of the situation. The problem is He doesn't always take the route we prefer... He's God and we're not. His perspective is oftentimes very different than ours.

I had to really grasp the concept of what He was saying about who I am now as opposed to who I used to be. I spend time with God because He is utterly amazing and there is no one like Him. He likes me for who I am. I don't have to explain myself to Him and hope He gets me. I don't have to impress Him to get Him to like me. He likes me because He knows things about me that I don't even know about myself. He loves helping me discover new things about myself. He enjoys my company. He's funny. He cares about me more than anyone else on the planet (even myself). He has my best interest at heart. His love is so warm and kind; very tenderhearted. He is soooooo creative ... very insightful... He has astounding wisdom!

You can't spend quality time with someone like that and not get better... My callous heart toward mean and ruthless people had softened; I have a growing compassion for them now. Usually, cold, hardened hearts arise from fear and abuse. No one who knows genuine love holds on to a cold, hardened heart; they cannot coexist. Having a hardened heart towards someone is usually backed by very good "excuses" for why we feel the way we do. Those excuses are the validation for why we're right and they're wrong, but these armored excuses also build fortresses that protect the hardened heart and keep it in the same cyclic state of callousness. True, genuine love repels a cold heart; it gravitates towards the warmth of true love and endeavors to protect that place of warmth and vitality.

I wanted to hold on to that heart of love that is so powerful, so warm and so strong, but yet so tender for the smallest need, but at the same time have a selfish Sylvester Stallone, Rambo moment. God sees where we really are and loves us anyway.

TRUE LOVE LIVES

True, genuine love is never about self. God was showing me something that was still residing on the inside of me, which I would have to willfully give up. I could simply do what He said, let that old identity die and step into the reality of the new identity that had been fashioned for me, or die to the next level of who I am in Him.

I did not want to remain a street-minded thug in response to any deliberately abrasive situation that was thrown at me. I wanted to be like the one Who I love the most—Papa God... I wanted to be like Him and do what He asked of me. There is no one who has given up so much for me and loved me so unconditionally. He's only ever wanted the absolute very best for me and He'd do whatever it takes to get me there—as long as I was willing...

I love looking at the magnitude of the endless details of creation. The photos from the International Space Station are astounding. He said He's numbered every hair on my head. We are as intricately designed as He has designed the universe, if not more, being made in His image and likeness. How much more does He care for the details of the desires of our hearts? His creation is just a minuscule display of the intricate depth of Who He is; you know an artist by their artistry. Being His workmanship, out of all that He could create us like unto, He created us like unto Himself.

His creativity is beyond comprehension... His best for me is completely above and beyond anything that I could ever imagine, ask or think. So, if He is saying who He is in me at this point in my life is far greater than who I was in my own-self, left to my own means, far be it for me to argue with that... All I had to do was be willing.

Who I had become in Him was far greater than what I was leaving behind. People respond to everything out of self-identity. Our response etiquette comes from an inner self-reservoir. Self-perception fills the reservoir of life within us.

This is a link to just one of the many astounding photos from NASA's International Space Station on Instagram - http://instagram.com/p/xZPnavtPsi/ http://instagram.com/iss for more fabulous photos.

2 MIRROR MIRROR

DEFINING ROOTS

Television, movies, and commercials are always appealing to an inner identity within us all. These various forms of media always make an offer or have a solution to life's problems. They are created in the mind of the marketer that is telling us that they have the solution to a pain or problem we're having. They want us to see ourselves in the image of the persona they are projecting. All it takes is a hint of one or two things that we truly identify with or something that we desire to identify without of a pain or a passion. Hundreds of billions of dollars are made annually by marketing companies that have a key insight into the heart of the consumers. The heart is where our identity lies, with all the emotions attached to it.

When I was in college, I had a friend who worked as an image creator for a large record company. When a new artist joined the label, it was his job to create the public image of the artist—their clothes, their hair, their style, their persona. They created a marketable image to sell the music of the artist. Part of selling anything is selling an image that people identify with. When young people identify with a celebrity, they're seeing a part of themselves in that person that has become larger than life. Inwardly they're saying, *That's me; I can be like that.* They are identifying with a persona; be it fantasy or reality, there is an identity connection being made. For some, so much so that they literally take on the whole "perceived" identity of their loved celebrity, not realizing that most are not projecting themselves, but only a persona that was created for them by someone else. Major companies hire marketing teams to sell records or product. The celebrity is then left with an image they have to live up to that is not truly who they really are.

Talk shows that host a lot of celebrities are successful because the audience gets to see a momentary glimpse into the life of one they've esteemed so highly. On a televised interview, one is able to validate their perceived identity of that person. *Are they really who I think they are? Are they as cool as they seem? I really relate to them, are they really just like me?* These are some of the inner, unspoken queries that go on initially within ourselves as we view our favorite celebrities for the first time in their unscripted interviews.

Who and what we identify with is what comes from our inner person. We speak out of the inner being of our hearts. The wealth of that inner-self comes from all that we hear, see and connect with over the years of our lives from childhood throughout adulthood. We draw from the people, places, and things that we identify with and that we long for in our hearts. There's a mirror reflection going on.

Having American Indian in my background, I saw myself as a warrior; along with being raised in the inner cities of Los Angeles, that had its elements of the thug life, I readily identified a fight to look like a street brawl—last man standing wins. I instinctively responded out of what I connected and identified with inwardly. We all do.

Actors will tell you the same thing. In order to portray a character skillfully on screen, they have to identify with and connect with the character they're portraying to give a performance that seems real to life. If the actor has no connection with that character, it shows. The heart of the audience is saying, "That's not real." The audience is unable to make a heart connection with it. The audience wants to be able to identify with what they're seeing on screen. They want to see themselves in one of the characters; one of which they can say, "I get them. I know why they do what they do." That is the voice of the inner identifier.

Our inner posture, temperament and attitude come from what we perceive ourselves to be and how we see ourselves... We reflect to others how we inwardly see ourselves. Who we perceive ourselves to be and who we actually are, does not necessarily have to be one and the same. Oftentimes it's not.

There is a great profile assessment by Tony Robbins (https://www.tonyrobbins.com/ue/disc-profile.php) that not only shows you the category of your persona but also how you actually see yourself through the eyes of others. The assessment is based on how you would normally respond and how you would respond based on how you think others expect you to respond. This is a great assessment because they both reflect different facets of self-perception. This particular test explains how they should be one and the same, but frequently they're not. They show you the variance to help you have a clearer perspective of yourself.

Tom Rath wrote a book called Strength Finders. Excellent book. When you purchase the book there is an assessment test by Gallup that profiles your top five strengths for your awareness and application that makes you stand out from others.

WHO AM I ANY REALLY?

Sometimes we are so used to "how we are", the way that we do things, that we don't really see "who we are", why we do the things we do. I did not wear makeup as a teenager or young adult. I did not wear lipstick or mascara until I was 21 years old and then it was at the coercion of my employer. I could not wait tables unless I wore lipstick and mascara; which I almost opted out of.

From my perspective, makeup was for girls who wanted to attract guys, and that was not me. I was not trying to attract guys at all. As a matter of fact, I preferred them to stay away. It was not until I was in my forties (yes, after 14 years of marriage and 3 children) that I actually began to wear makeup, beyond the must-wear on Sundays for church. At my wedding, one of my guests came and put make-up on me that she had in her purse for my wedding photos. She was standing by, watching us take photos, and noticed I didn't have a bit of make-up on at all. That childhood perception in my heart carried on through my adult life because it went unresolved.

It was always said, "Oh, that's just Robyn. Plain Jane," and so, plain Jane I was. I thought simple was better; less complicated. The problem with this scenario is that I did not identify "plain Jane" or simplicity with beauty. I identified simplicity with safety. For me, there was safety in the down-play of self. To be made up and beautified was to draw attention to myself, of which I was dreadfully afraid. Growing up, I was shy beyond cuteness. Some would think shyness was cute; for me, shyness had fear attached to it.

The emotion attached to what you identify with is a great indicator of the role it plays in your life. Next time you catch yourself identifying with someone or something, notice the emotion attached to it. Then you will see it surface in other areas of your life when that emotion is triggered. (This is useful to know when you find your true identity to help negate a false identity that is to be replaced by the true.)

Growing up, I was so far removed from self, I could not identify my true self, my likes or dislikes. I was almost neutral when it came to a perception of myself. I had no likes nor did I have any dislikes. This was because I did not know my true self nor did I find value in getting to know my true self. At some point in my life, I identified with invisibility. Invisible is safe. Some defining roots had been exposed. From this perspective, I could either fight to remain hidden or find my true self and learn to love who God made me to be.

All that comes out of God and remains is good. Showing the true you to yourself is God's part, remaining true to the real you is our part. All of mankind came out of God, not just those of Christian faith. Yes, even the person that calls himself an atheist was made in the image and likeness of God.

God loves him so much He gave him the power of choice; the freedom to choose or not to choose a relationship with God if that's what he wants. It doesn't negate the fact that he was still created from the image of God. An atheist's unbelief in God does not change his origin. He or she originated from the image and likeness of God. We are all people, born a person, created from the image of God before we could ever make a decision for or against Him.

He made man in His image and after His likeness. Christianity came thousands of years after God made man. The image of man has always had the capability of mirroring the image of God. The issue remains with man, are you reflecting who He created you to be or mirroring an image created by others?

If we identify with all that our culture is about, that is what we will speak from and this is how our choices are made. Our cultural root system that defines us can be good or not so good. What we identify with within ourselves is what we will respond out of. All those who are born of the Spirit of the living God are of the culture of the Kingdom of God. Being born of His Spirit offers a greater capacity to live out the image we were created from than simply being created from His likeness; there's a difference. There is relationship in being born of His Spirit, which does not come from just being created like Him.

Problems arise when we identify with a culture that is contrary to His Kingdom; contrary to the very image we were born out of. No matter how hard we try to fit in and make it work, if it's not from Him we will ultimately feel empty and insignificant.

"If you want to know the purpose of a product, you must ask the manufacturer or his authorized representative. The product itself cannot tell you." – Dr. Myles Munroe

THE NATURAL ROYALS KNOW BETTER

Can you see Kate from the British royal family in a street brawl? I think not... Natural, earthly royals know how to conduct themselves in any situation. I'm sure there was some level of training that she was given in how to conduct herself as becoming a part of the royal family.

There is a certain standard of conduct and demeanor that one has in being of royal linage. It is time we identify with our Creator and draw from the strength of who we really are. There is strength to be found in our true identity. We are a part of a royal linage of the Kingdom of God. Getting to know that part of our heritage will help us to think differently about ourselves.

"What you are and how you are was predetermined by why you are." – Dr. Myles Munroe

I AM WHO I THINK I AM

Man has always asked the questions, "Why am I here?" "What's my purpose?" We try to "become" what we've seen in others; particularly when we're not happy with how we see ourselves or what we're becoming. As my kids (actually young adults now) have often said, "The struggle is real." As a man thinks in his heart, so is he. We become who we perceive ourselves to be.

With her permission, I'd like to share a paper on The Source of Identity that was written by a beautiful, twelve-year-old girl named Anekah Smith.

The Source of Identity

Sometimes I feel very uncomfortable when I see people look at me in a way that tells me they're uncomfortable with looking at my skin. I've had so many doctors' appointments and prescriptions, I can't even begin to count them. I have this skin condition called eczema which is inflammation of the skin with severe itching that comes with it. It's very severe right now, but that is kind of my fault because I don't take very good care of my skin (consistently) like I am supposed to. Sometimes when I'm around little kids and they ask, "What's on your skin?" I feel more and more insecure about myself, but during those times I've always known I have God's help to get me through and I know He always has my back.

Identity is a term of important meaning yet simply can be considered a specific person or thing with their own unique attributes. Oftentimes, the world bases your identity on outward things like status or beauty, when what is really important is what and who's inside—an inner beauty. In psalm 139 verses 13-16 it says, "Oh yes, I shaped you first inside, then out; I formed you in your mother's womb." That is where my identity begins! To that I say, "Thank you, High God—you're breathtaking!" Body and soul, I am marvelously made! I worship my God in adoration— and marvel "What a creation!" You know me inside and out, you know every bone in my body; you know exactly how I was made, bit by bit, how I was sculpted from nothing into something. Like an open book, you watched me grow from conception to birth; all the stages of my life were spread out before you. The days of my life all prepared before I'd even lived one day." (Psalm 139:13-16 MSG)

This is a fact and the Truth; that He made me inside then out, He knows what I'm going to do, say, and think. He knows every bit of me, how I feel and what my hair looks like. Isn't that amazing? God loves all of his children, not just me or you—everybody! And He loves us all exactly the same no matter what! In the scripture, it says He has a plan for us and He knows what we're going to be and knows what we're going to do; He knows everything—even what we're going to do for a living. I believe I am a child of God, perfect in His image. No matter what the world says about how I'm supposed to look, God already has planned out what He has in store for me. I thank God for giving me such a unique identity, I might feel small some moments but God always has my back.

Anekah, at a very young age, has set a course for her life in realizing the importance of identity and self-worth. She went to the very root system of her existence and plotted her course. Acknowledging the author of her existence and recognizing her value based on Who created her, empowered her to have a perception of strength in the course of life's dealings.

There are plenty of life stories of people who were rich but lost it all and, in no time, became rich all over again because, inwardly, they never saw themselves as poor. How you choose to see yourself inwardly is the fuel for living your life effectively or non-effectively. The same is true with some who grew up in poverty with a poverty mindset; money was given to them and, in a short period of time, they became poor all over again. External things do not change who we are, they are reflective of our identity and self-worth. To change external situations, we must begin within.

Far too often, we want to escape from ourselves and be someone else. We think the grass is greener in someone else's backyard. When someone's heart is weighed down with negative thoughts about himself, when he looks in the mirror he is incapable of seeing any good. The heart of his inner man is tainted with rays of darkness from the weight and the perception of negative thoughts. That is why so many books have been written about "positive thinking". It is scientifically proven that negative thoughts emit darkness and despair. This darkness impairs one's perception.

There is a blog post called Toxic Thoughts, by Dr. Caroline Leaf. She states, "75% to 95% of the illnesses that plague us today are a direct result of our thought life." Dr. Caroline Leaf is a cognitive neuroscientist with a Ph.D. in Communication Pathology specializing in Neuropsychology. She says what we think about affects us physically and emotionally.

Dr. Leaf further states, "Medical research increasingly points to the fact that thinking and consciously controlling your thought life is one of the best ways, if not the best way of detoxing your brain. It allows you to get rid of those toxic thoughts and emotions that can consume and control your mind." My website www.lifeinHim.us has a list of helpful resource books, blog posts, YouTube videos and teaching on this.

When we first wake up in the morning and go to the bathroom, we usually turn on the light and then look in the mirror to assess the work that it's going to take to get us looking great for a new day. Naturally speaking, dimmed lighting impairs sight. At night, we drive with our headlights on. When I go out to a restaurant for dinner, I am not into the dimmed, romantic lighting so much. I want to see very well what I'm eating.

There was one Mexican food restaurant that my family and I used to go to and I just sulked whenever we went there because I hated the lighting. To me, the dimmed lighting wasn't romantic mood lighting; it was just plain ole dark! The ambiance was ruined because I couldn't see my food.

It is easy to let excuses and creative reasoning dim the perspective of ourselves in our own hearts. When we can't or don't see ourselves as we were created to be, we want what we think someone has or to be who we think they are. Maybe all we need to do is turn the light up a bit more on ourselves to see the goodness and value in what we already have.

LIKE ME; LOVE ME

There is a gentleman named Nick Vujicic who was born with no legs and no arms. In this extraordinary situation, he could have been inhibited for life. He once felt his life was pointless; thinking he would never be able to go to school or university. He says, "What's the point of being complete on the outside when you're broken on the inside? What's the point of holding your wife's hand when you can't hold her heart?" He now swims, surfs, snorkels, golfs and even plays soccer.

As Nick's story goes, he came home from school one day when he was six years old, hurt and upset. He couldn't sleep that night from being tormented by the kids teasing and taunting him at school. He got up from his bed and went to the bathroom mirror. He asked himself what he had that was good, that no one could argue with. There had to be something. What was it? It was his eyes. He realized he had great eyes. He uses his eyes to talk to people. He lets people see love and joy in his eyes. He had a royal change of mind about himself. Regardless of any bad lot in life we may seem to have, we all have something beautiful that can be shared with others.

As a young girl in the 5th or 6th grade, I heard one of my friends sing for the very first time. I remember thinking how talented she was. Wow, I didn't know that was in her. She looked at me as if to say, "Don't you sing, too?" I just smiled and thought *I hope she doesn't ask me to sing with her!* In that moment, I felt so boring and worthless. It was nothing she had done. I just felt like there was some talent that I was supposed to have but I didn't. Have you ever felt that way before?

Nick could have also felt a sense of worthlessness at some point in his life because everyone else around him had arms and legs. All of my friends could sing and dance; I couldn't do either.

A sense of worthlessness can stem from not having something that is valuable. I was very awkward and couldn't carry a tune in a bucket, as the saying goes. I was ok in sports, but no special talent there because it held very little interest for me.

I always excelled in school. I had to excel in school because of the standards my parents held me to; I had to do exceptionally well. To me, everyone could do that, study hard get good grades. Getting excellent grades in school was not special to me. I didn't see where any talent was needed for that.

Sometimes a gift is so natural that it's hard to detect. I felt like all of my friends had "talent" and I had none. All of my friends did well in school, but they had something I didn't, they had talent. In my eyes, that made them more valuable than me.

The artist in me had yet to be discovered. It was hidden in the shadows of academia. Well, we all have something special about us, we just need to explore some other interests a little more, and it will surface. Don't let inabilities obscure your capabilities. There's plenty to love about you.

Back to Nick. Nick Vujicic realized everyone is going through something. His was just more visible than everyone else's. Nick learned how to make the best of what he had been dealt in life. Choosing not to be restricted by what many would call a handicap, he sought out the good in what he did have. He has traveled the world bringing hope to others. He is now married and has a baby boy. Check out his YouTube channel, Nick Vujicic TV. This clip from Oprah Winfrey's show is an amazing must see. http://youtu.be/YwpiZTpON9k

3 WHO KNEW?

WILL THE REAL YOU PLEASE STAND UP?

In my opinion, the greatest phenomenon of all time is to be made in the very image and likeness of God. What does that really look like? Jim Cavezel did an amazing job of playing Jesus in the Passion of The Christ by Mel Gibson. Jesus said, "When you've seen Me you've seen the Father." History has shown us all sorts of variations of Jesus, from an artist's perspective. Could one of those renditions be what God looks like?

I look like a great mix of my dad and my mom. Does that mean all of mankind should favor each other and look like brother and sisters if we all came out of God? Well, that whole pattern of thought is very understandable. Actually, I am not my physical body and neither are you. Just like God, we are all spirits. Living here on earth, our spirit resides inside of a physical body.

I have three children. My oldest daughter's name is Daven. If I were to say, "Oh, that's not Daven," in response to a loud, obnoxious description of her, I would not be referring to her physical body; I would be talking about her as a person. That description did not fit who I know her to be as a person. Daven is very reserved and somewhat soft spoken. If someone said she was loud, boisterous and obnoxious, I would know they did not know her or may have gotten her confused with someone else who might physically look like her. Daven's heart and persona, even when she's upset, remains the same—cool, calm and collected. Even when upset, she never goes above a 5 on a scale of 1-10.

I was a hands-on mom. I spent quality time with my children. I know their personalities well enough to know when someone is describing something out of character for them. Also, I am very aware of the strengths and weaknesses of their character that could lead to something out of the ordinary for each of them.

To know what God "looks like" is to know God's heart, who He really is, like you would know someone who is very close to you. You can only truly know someone if you spend time with them.

Descriptive information about them does not reveal the heart of who they truly are. What people say about you does not make you who you are. Although we all should strive for excellence of character, we can't let negative things people say to and about us from a heart of negativity affect how we see ourselves.

Many people have said many things about God. I would venture to say that the arbitrary things people have said about Him are not true. They are usually things based on hearsay, rarely from a true life experience. It is very easy to have an opinion about someone and not have to validate the information or it's source.

I went to Catholic school from 1st grade through 12th grade. We had church weekly and religion classes every semester.

Needless to say, I had a lot of information "about" God. Given the source, it's easy to assume that they know what they're talking about. Being the inquisitive one that I was, when it came to things about God, I really wanted to know the truth. I had a lot of questions. Everything had to add up. If it didn't, I had even more questions.

My hunger and pursuit of God drew me to my neighbor next door who had a "relationship" with God. One day, she asked if I "knew" Jesus. Well, of course I did, what Catholic school girl does not "know who Jesus is"? That really wasn't her question. What she was really asking me was did I know Him or did I know "about" Him.

That simple inquiry led me to say a prayer on the phone with a preacher on the radio. After I prayed a simple prayer to accept the price that Jesus paid for everything I had done wrong in my life, Mr. Clark, the gentleman on the radio, offered to send me a Bible. It was my first very own, personal Bible. I was so excited because the big, white Catholic family Bible we had was very intimidating. No one ever said I had to read it, but I thought, if I wanted to get to know God, I should. It was too big and heavy to get comfortable reading. I had to leave it on the coffee table just to open it up. The pictures were interesting to look at but the one where Abraham was putting Isaac on the chopping block was a bit much for me. That was the end of that Bible.

When my Bible from Mr. Clark came, I would spend hours every day in my room reading it and asking God questions. I was only thirteen years old. No one told me that you couldn't talk to God. I had a lot of questions and I figured He was the one to ask. I did not know where anything was in the Bible. All I knew was Genesis is at the beginning and Revelation is at the end. I didn't know how to find anything else, so I'd just ask God my questions, open my Bible and there was the answer. He'd answer my questions that way quite often and then sometimes He'd just answer them on the inside of me.

Now, at this point, I didn't know anything about Christianity nor very much about Catholicism either. I loved just sitting talking to God. His presence was very kind, loving and fun. I did not have any religious template to tell me what I could or couldn't do. I was free to be me and He was free to be Himself without any rules and regulations.

A year later, I was introduced to this Christian Bible church. At that time, I had only been to Catholic mass and a few Baptist Sunday services.

I went to this new church with my mom and her friend who had invited us. I loved it straight from the start. Everything the minister was saying, God had talked to me about at home! This was great! It became my new home church. I went to that church for 19 years. Although it was a great Bible teaching church, I slowly began to let "church" take the place of my time with God. Sad to say, I had to re-cultivate a relationship with God later on down the line.

Church is great, but it can never take the place of God in your life. Far too often theology and church life begin to dictate to us who God is. Spending time with Him is essential to knowing Him because He knows how to make Himself known to us. Give Him an opportunity to be Himself in your life and you'll begin to get a glimpse of yourself through His eyes. Only He knows the real you.

It's like when a guy marries the girl of his dreams. They were dating for so long and pursuing one another. Their hearts are consumed with one another until, one day, they decide they want to live the rest of their lives together forever; they decide to get married.

Well, as anyone who has been married for any length of time knows, if that initial fire in the marriage is not attentively cared for, life itself can get in the way of the two love birds and they begin to grow apart and they do not know how or why.

That's what happened with my relationship with the Lord. Church life happened and sitting still and just enjoying God's company grew far and few between until it became awkward. My time had become filled with the busyness of church life.

God didn't go anywhere, I did. We have as much of God as we want. He is not going to force Himself on anyone. He will pursue you then you will have the opportunity to accept or reject His pursuit. He's done His part, the ball always remains in our court. He gives us enough to step out on; if we don't move in that direction it stops there, and He will kindly and patiently wait for us. He never turns His back on us. It's we who do the back turning. He said, "Draw near to Me and I will draw near to you."

I share all of this so that you know of my relationship with the Lord. That when I say there is a difference between knowing about God and knowing Him I have lived a life of great experiences with Him and still do.

Spending great quality time with God, letting Him be Himself in my life, inevitably allowed me to see myself as He sees me. This is where I began to have a better perspective of myself and others. As I said earlier, you can't spend time with someone and not be changed by them. Again, you are a reflection of your five closest friends. (I don't know where that particular number comes from, but, suffice to say, you become like who you associate with.)

Spending time with God gives you strength to step out with boldness and confidence. You begin to identify with your true heritage, who you really are.

I have some really great, supernatural experiences with God and tons of very normal life experiences with Him. I am struck with awe when I stop and just ponder and think about being made in His image and likeness. His awesomeness stupefies me. To stop and ponder being crafted from the vastness of God can be a bit much to fathom. We have so much untapped potential it can be almost insulting to God that we don't embrace it.

Who we really are, made from His image and His persona, really needs to step forward in our lives. If no one points it out; how are we to know? This book is about stirring an awakening within you the reader because you're made in the image and likeness of God, there is so much more to you than you could ever imagine. I challenge you to spend quality time with God that the greater you, that is made in His image, may live.

NO MARDI GRAS MASK FOR ME

Masks, no matter how you slice it, are for disguise only. Masks are never intended to show the true you. With the increase of media being at the hands of the consumer, more so than ever been before, it has become cool and trendy to create, design and hide behind a vast amount of creativity, through the guise of photo filters. Take a look at the huge array of the app filters that are available. For today's social media, filters are the accepted norm. For a genuinely creative photo, you have to write #nofilter for one to know that was the actual photo taken. Why? Because it's a given that, if it's a great photo with very creative color, there has to be a filter on it.

Filters are fantastic. I love playing with them. They create and initiate mood. You can look through an assortment of filters to put on your photo and go from a swoon to a cringe just from the shift of a photo filter. Filters are dynamically ingenious.

Problems arise when we use filters to self-protect our hearts from the realities of life. These problems can grow worse when we move from filters to what I call the Mardi Gras mask stage. The filters of life do not allow us to see or be seen for who we really are. There is a thin line between creating a look that expresses your heart and creating a look that is masking your heart.

A filter designed to create a certain look or mood can be fun and expressive. When a filter is applied to our lives to give a false perception of the actual truth, that's where the danger is. It becomes a disguise instead of an enhancement.

When a woman dresses in '60s attire with the full make-up, heavy eyeliner, and falsie lashes, it's considered a "certain look". Some of us wear certain eras well and like to accentuate our attire or fill our entire wardrobe with that look. I love it. I personally love when someone can pull off an era and make it look modern. To me, that's the essence of fashion.

All fashion repeats itself on many levels. My children think ripped jeans and converse tennis shoes are cool. Well, yea, they're cool today, but they were also "cool" 30 years ago. Back then we only had three colors to choose from for our Converse, black, white and navy. Today, there's an assortment of colors to choose from but they're still the exact same shoe. We called them "All Stars", "Chucks" and "Converse", today, they're just "Converse". To my children 30 years ago is so old and so long ago, but that was what was in fashion then and has made its way back around to the pinnacle of teen young adult fashion once more, today.

When an era has pulled someone back in time and they don't realize what decade they're in, it speaks of an influence that has captured their heart to the point that they'd rather live there than in the present. It is now no longer a fashion statement but an identity issue.

It becomes an identity issue when we take personally what is said about us. It's no longer, "Oh, you don't like my skirt," or "You don't like my eye make-up," it has become, "You don't like me," "You think I'm weird," "You're just a hater," "You're judging me." These statements rise up because the inner self has become one with the image that the clothes or look represent. This is the dangerous part because we are all so much more than what we wear or how we look, yet what we wear and how we look says so much about who we are and what is going on in our lives.

I know for myself, and it is probably true for others as well, when I'm "feeling happy" about life I dress more fun, cool and hip. When I'm not feeling all that joyful about life, I don't care so much about what I put on and will just throw something together. As long as it matches, I'm good. Our attitude about ourselves speaks volumes about our identity. What we identify with triggers our response to life issues and day-to-day situations.

That false filter has the potential to grow into a mask of protection, a false protection. When I was in jr. high and high school I had a few gangster thug friends from my neighborhood. I went to Catholic school and had to wear a uniform, which was a saving grace. I had a mixed group of friends from my neighborhood. A Christian family lived in the back, a black Muslim family lived in the front and we were the non-practicing Christian family neighboring the side of these two families.

All three of us girls were the same age. We all had our "uniforms" that we wore during the week, each of which was the identifier with the culture of our established educational institutions.

When we were home and uniforms were put away, we all tried to identify with the culture of our neighborhood, your average middle-class neighborhood that had a few gang bangers splattered here and there. It was a nice, clean neighborhood but there was that unsavory element that was searching to establish its own place in society. Those were the newbie bangers that had to prove and establish themselves in their hood, a.k.a. their territory. They were great people who were greatly misunderstood by themselves and others. I didn't see them as bangers; I saw them as individuals.

There was a guy in our neighborhood named Mexican Moses who drove a "lowrider" car. Everyone was afraid of him. There was always talk about Mexican Moses circulating the neighborhood and the things that he had done. When I met him, I thought, *Wow, this is such a nice guy.* To this day, I don't know how much was hype and how much of the talk was true. I just remember from that day on thinking gang bangers were not as bad as people made them out to be. I found a place in my heart to empathize with those labeled by society as "no good". I felt as though each person is an individual and should be treated as such.

You won't know them until you take the time to get to know who they really are. I also found out that the gang bangers all wanted the same thing everyone else wanted, love and family. They just went about it a different way. Because of hurt and pain in their own families, they came into their gang community with many false walls and masks of protection; walls of anger, bitterness and rage to protect the hurt, wounded and painful areas of their lives. Deep down inside they were aspiring to an unknown greatness but not knowing how to get there.

No one is born aspiring to be the greatest loser in life. As I mentioned before, everyone is made in the image and likeness of God. There is a seed of greatness in each and every one of us. Labeling people not only segregates them from community but also separates us from the goodness that is to be found in each other.

Now, don't get me wrong, I know that there are people who have done some really horrible things in life. I still feel that if someone takes the time to find the goodness in them and cultivate that instead of the negative labels that we sometimes presume upon people, we can steer a life towards the potential greatness that resides inside of them.

God Himself said, "I have placed before you death and life, choose life that you and your seed may live." He's saying, I've given you two options in life and I am also giving you the answer to the two options; but I love you enough to give you the freedom to make your own choice. Identify with Me or identify with that which not only opposes Me but also opposes everything that I created you to be.

I personally know a few very wealthy people and a few major celebrities. These are great people who worked hard to obtain and achieve their various levels of success in life. But they all will tell you there is no success in life until you've hit that sweet spot in knowing that you're doing what you were "designed and created" to do. Neither the money nor the status is the sigh of relief that I've made it; the sigh of relief comes from knowing I'm doing what I was created for.

From teens to young adults to middle-aged adults, there are plenty of people still asking the same, age-old question:

"What am I here for? Who am I and what was I created to do?" There is an inner completion that is satisfied when certain things are accomplished or achieved that you were destined to do or be. Neither money nor status can give you that. It's an inner hunger in the DNA of our spirit that has to be fulfilled, or we'll die empty and unfulfilled.

Living in the guise of someone else never allows you to fulfill who you actually were created to be; so many have lost themselves in the false masks of protection, correctness, perfection and false identity. These masks have been used to protect us from a perceived hurt or pain. The masks of correctness and perfection make us feel as though there is an unbearable affliction of pain to endure if we're not correct or perfect, so whether we are or not we will mask it as though we are. The mask is an illusion of a false identity looking for acceptance and inclusion.

We shouldn't be so hard on ourselves. The only perfect one is Jesus. It required Him Who knew no sin to become sin for us. He had to have a sinless life to pay for lives that were riddled with sin. Since God is God, He was the only One who could set the standard by which judgment for sin is to be paid. The creation (which we are) could not come up with its own rules and standards by which to live and be judged by. It was already set in place before we got here. He carried the weight of perfection for us. His grace allows for us to strive for excellence that His perfection paid for.

It's the same with us before we recognized that we could sing, dance, act, excel academically, be a great orator, engineer, doctor, lawyer or chemist, etc. it was already in us as a seed that had to be cultivated and nurtured to maturity. Who and what we are today are the seeds of our lives that were put in the right ground with the right environment, watered, cultivated and nurtured to maturity. Giving ourselves permission to grow allows for peace in the process. Peace yields love and together they dispel the fear that falsifies.

When we seek the creator of a thing, we find the purpose for which it was created; otherwise, "where purpose is unknown abuse is inevitable," as I again quote Dr. Myles Munroe. What am I saying? It's only God who can reveal to us the true purpose for which each of us was created. Knowing our purpose brings peace.

In order to remove a mask, we must first know that it's there and be willing to relinquish it. Realizing it's there can be difficult because we've either had it for so long, and we don't want to let go of what we've grown attached to, or we've so identified with it that it has amalgamated into our own true identity.

Mardi Gras masks are colorful and inviting. They're whimsical and fun. Who wouldn't want one? No matter how grand the cover up is, it's still a cover up. The questions that need to be answered are what is it covering and why? Truth is, living a false identity has its roots in fear and shame. In order to properly eradicate something, it must be pulled up from the root. Just cutting off branches and fruit only suffices for the moment; the branches and fruit grow back.

We were designed to be unashamed. When we identify with being wrong, we want to cover it up or make it right. Why? There's shame associated with being wrong. If we didn't think something was wrong with us, we wouldn't want to change ourselves to become someone else.

If we think there's something wrong with us, we will also feel a loss in value. When I thought that there was something wrong with me because I had no talent, along with those feelings of inadequacy came shame and loss of value.

Everyone has felt this at some point in their lives, some on a larger scale than others, but we've all experienced an identity crisis with a need for masking.

If you are a parent like I am, you can see the strengths, abilities, and weaknesses in your children at a very young age. All three of my children are now beginning to grow and flourish in what God has created them for. God placed them in the right family at the right time for their strengths and abilities to emerge and give face and identity to what had been there all along. Sometimes we can't see the forest for the trees, but yet it's the trees that make the forest.

I remember complaining to God one day about what I didn't get in life and if my parents would just have given me piano lessons and nurtured my desire to play, I wouldn't be taking piano lessons as an adult and pining over what I could have become (in my own mind). I will never forget His response to me. He told me that I am who I am today because of everything that I got and everything I didn't get. He also said for me to know the value of what I currently have I needed to have a thankful heart. He was showing me the value of what I did have in my life was hidden from me because of thanklessness.

If I valued what I had right there in the moment, I would be able to see its greatness. Being thankful towards what I have thus far is key to becoming fulfilled and fruitful in all I was created to be.

In that moment of love rebuke from Papa God, I called my parents and my grandfather to thank them for all they did for me in my life and how much I appreciate them.

I called my grandfather because, in that moment, I remembered how much he sacrificed of his life for my dad to go to a private boarding school in high school. That was a major accomplishment for an African American in the south during the '50s. What he did for my dad then contributed to who he became, which, in turn, contributed to who I had become in that moment and what was yet still emerging.

The Lord also said that if I had taken the classes that I thought I should have, it would have affected how I raised my children. The music in me was a catalyst for them today. All three of them are in the perfect place today for their gifts to flow freely for what and who they were created to be.

If I had pruned my children in such a way to fulfill my own personal unfulfilled dreams in life, that could, and most times would be very damaging to them. So often parents groom their kids to be what they never could or did become themselves. I love where my children are and what they're doing. They are in the creative arts from design to music to production. My perspective of what I wanted or what I could have been would have been far limiting for them as well as for myself.

God's vision for the artist in me has blossomed into and is still in the process of, building a military boarding school for students in the arts. His vision for us is always above and beyond what we would image, hope or think. What we're doing and what He's shown me for the school is beyond the stratosphere of what I would have ever imaged for myself. What He has for us is always to reach others. We can sometimes be so self-absorbed. Far too often our own vision is for selfish gain or from an insecurity that is seeking approval from others.

When parents are living their lives through the life of their children, as though it's their second go around in life to get what they missed earlier, it's futile. This is very damaging on so many levels, for the child as well as for the adult.

One, you can't live "your" life through your child's life. It's theirs and theirs alone to live out and to become. They were created for their own greatness to be achieved.

Secondly, that is still living for fulfillment through someone else and not looking inwardly for what God has placed inside of you to have its own expression. What it's really saying is, "I'm not all that great, but you are." The root of that thought is shame and inadequacy. It's telling you that you need to be like someone else to achieve any level of significance or greatness. That is living your life through the lens of someone else's strengths and successes.

Our strengths and also our weaknesses make us who we are. The combination of the two, coupled with our life experiences and our response to them, gives us our individual uniqueness. Looking at life through the rear view mirror or, even worse, someone else's mirror, would cause one to miss out on what they truly were created to be.

BONSAI NOT I

Seeds will remain seeds until they are planted in the right environment with the correct nutrition and nourishment. A plant also must be properly pruned as it grows.

I remember going to a really beautiful garden museum in a city close to where I live. They have twelve gardens from all over the world. There is a Japanese garden that features bonsai plants. Bonsai plants are miniature trees that were specifically grown and pruned to be miniature versions of their mature state. They are grown to about 12-24 inches in height when in actuality they were created to be 20-30 feet or taller. They are fascinating to see. A full grown tree just two feet tall, sitting tabletop. A real tree that is supposed to tower over you is sitting in a potted container on a table.

I knew of them, but to see them in person was very intriguing yet horrifically disturbing to me. I realized it was disturbing to me because I identified with this full grown tree that was contained and potted. Its growth had been deliberately stunted. Wikipedia says, "Bonsai can be created from nearly any perennial woody-stemmed tree or shrub species that produces true branches and can be cultivated to remain small through pot confinement with crown and root pruning."

For years I did not know why I identified with this tree, I just knew I did. After seeing the bonsai tree in person, I hated the very thought of them. Why would I identify with this tree?

I was married with three children. Life had its ups and downs but it was still good. I had a growing jewelry company with several specialty boutique clients and two Saks Fifth Avenue stores, on both the east and west coast. Why was I feeling like my growth had been deliberately stunted? (Well, the truth of that story is a whole other book in itself.) I felt as though I was flourishing, but what was this? A bonsai looks mature and grown, but in comparison to what it's supposed to look like, it's very dwarfed.

Since that time, God has placed me in an environment that cultivates and prunes the gifts to their full maturity. This new atmosphere was breathing life back into me. There is a saying, "Don't judge your chapter one by someone else's chapter twenty." When you feel as though you've been on the chapter one of your life for twenty years, it can be disturbing. God has a way of getting you to the exact place you need to be at the right time.

One of the things I've learned over the years, there is nothing so horrific that God cannot and will not love you through. I remember at one point in my life thinking that He had to really be done with me at that point. There had to be far better people to work with.

I remember Him telling me not to be so disturbed over the wrong choices in my life; He was using them as compost! I was so excited! That was liberating for me. I no longer saw myself as a failure, but one who He could use, regardless of how imperfect I was. God would use all of my bad choices as organic fertilizer! He is brilliant beyond brilliant! I love how He thinks! He's like, "Don't worry about it, just keep going."

Know this, if there is anything in your life that makes you feel like you have completely ruined everything, God is not afraid, upset or bothered by it, He's just looking for you to be willing to change and willing to obey, He'll take care of the rest.

Since God is outside of time, He sees every mistake coming before we do and He already has a plan of how to factor the upsets of life into working together for our good when we remain set to do what we were designed and created to do. There is no failure in Him. He just makes it all work out. I love that about Him. Freedom in Him waters and prunes our lives to full maturity in all we were created to be.

TRUE FRIENDS LOVE AT ALL TIMES

Wisdom has taught me over the years to seek the good in each person. That doesn't mean that each person is to be embraced in your inner circle; a wise man chooses his friends carefully. You'll find what you're looking for pessimistically or optimistically.

Something that I found out as an adult, and that I wished I had known in my teenage years, is the benefit of establishing a criterion for every level of friendship in my life. If you don't, every nice and funny person will qualify. Nice and funny are great qualifiers but have very broad strokes in the orchestration of life. To use a finer scope, look at what people value, how they spend their time, and who the most important people are in their life and why.

Favorite movies, music, art, cars and countries are all so subjective and do not reveal the core of the person. I always tell my kids to look at how their friends honor their parents. If there is a problem in that area, they will have a problem with authority. If they have a problem with authority, they will inevitably veer off of a proper course in their life and find trouble.

Authority is not always correct. If we honor those in authority because of their position, not because they're always right, God will make sure it works well for us because He will have our back. I have lived by this principle for years and it has helped me weather many storms.

When you have friends who value you and you value them, there is no need for masks. There is trust because of the established value for one another. You don't have to be made to respect and esteem someone you value. You are free to be yourself with each other because the fear of condemnation is removed.

When you want the best for each other you will not feel the need to compete with each other. We give to what we value. People take from and diminish what they hold in low esteem. Competition sometimes makes people strive harder, but it can also make people falsify who they really are. People use a protective mask, fearing who they really are does not measure up or will be rejected or fail.

Fear is the culprit behind the false masks of identity. The greater the fear the greater the masquerade. The Mardi Gras masks come out when one's value is trying to be established. Validation substantiates our value. Fear of worthlessness provokes one to falsify value. To alleviate fear, love has to be present. The genuineness of our family and friends is crucial to our self-worth.

I had a really amazing friend in my life at one time. I thought there was absolutely nothing this woman could not do. Absolutely the most incredible artist I have ever met, and she has awards of global recognition to prove it. She's the type of person who knows how to look past your weaknesses and draw out your strengths. My quirkiness did not bother her. She loved how much I loved the Lord. Life was grand. I love, love, love this woman. Even though today we're not where we used to be because life has steered us in different directions, I still have an enduring affectionate love in my heart for her.

One day, my beautiful friend and I went on a trip to Canada. At this point, we had been the best of best friends. We were both so very excited about our trip and the adventure we were on. She was always the one to introduce me to new levels of exploration and adventure.

After dinner one night, she told me that she wanted to help me with something and that I was going to have to trust her on this. I was thinking, *Trust her, she knows my whole life, what would I not trust her with?* I agreed and went along with the program. She proceeded to tell me that I had been wearing a mask and that she wanted to remove it. I was in shock. Me? Wearing a mask? I had no reason to wear a mask, particularly not with her. I am a very candid person.

My thought was that masks were deceptive and I did not need to hide behind a mask. I didn't think I had a mask at all with anyone, but especially not with her. But I trusted her, I knew she loved me and always wanted the best for me, so I obliged and followed along. She prayed for me and proceeded to remove the (invisible) mask. As she did that, something happened; I was able to feel the transparency that had just taken place. Very interesting thing to experience.

She recognized a protective mask in place that was hiding a facet of my true identity. In her love for me, approaching with love and caution, she removed the mask of protection so another facet of my true self could feel free to emerge in a safe place. True friends love you enough to walk with you through your strengths and weaknesses. They will not let you remain hidden. They see the treasure in you and draw it out.

I have another great story about this beautiful friend of mine, whose name is Cathy. She was helping me with producing my first CD. We were taking my photos for the cover.

That familiar, protective, shy mask wanted to emerge but it was Cathy, so I let her take the photos. What did I do that for? She captured the one and only photo of me that actually reveals the core of my true self. I did not like that picture. I did not want to use it.

People could "see me". There was a look on my face that no one had ever seen before, at least, I thought not. Most assuredly, Cathy had. I tried desperately to keep that part of me hidden. She insisted and said that it was time that people saw the real me.

Again, I trusted her and we used the photo. We actually ended up using it as the photo for the inside of my CD cover.

That was another revealing moment in a safe place, but this time, it went public.

Cathy knew me well enough to know when and how to draw out the true Robyn that was still hidden inside. People who value you will draw that value out to be shared with others. That's where you'll find true joy. That's how God made us. Our lives were meant to be shared with others, not hidden out of fear of rejection or pain.

True value for someone is a peacemaker for true self to emerge. My friend Cathy saw value in me and drew it out for others to see. God saw what He had made and said it was good. That includes you. You are worthy of His attention. When the true you calls out to Him, He turns and listens.

YOU WEAR IT WELL

You may not yet feel comfortable in your own skin, but it came custom made from God Himself and it's a perfect fit. Sometimes we've grown so accustomed to the old clothes of our old identity that we don't recognize the attractiveness of our true selves. It's like wearing a hairstyle for several years. You know you need a change but you've grown so used to seeing yourself with a certain look that a new change would be so foreign to you it would be a culture shock.

My husband died suddenly. It was unexpected. He was sick but we didn't know it, and when he passed away it was a shock to everyone. He was here one day and gone the next. We were married for fourteen years. The suddenness of it was mentally difficult to handle. I remember nothing around me seemed real. I wasn't sure if the couch I was sitting on while talking to people about what had just happened was real. I kept looking at it to see if it was still there.

My sister, Roz, was a hairstylist at the time. For the funeral, she wanted to change my hairstyle, give me a new look, thinking this might help to cheer me up. I freaked out. I didn't want her touching my hair.

Everything had to stay the same. I wouldn't change the phone recording. I wouldn't move or change anything in the house. My identity changed in one day and it was all too shocking to embrace all at once.

God knows what you need before you do. My friend Audrey came in and changed my entire bedroom. She took me shopping for new furniture, bedding, paint and all. The intimate place in my home had been redesigned with all of my own personal choices.

My friend Cathy, who I spoke of before, had me go in the refrigerator and make a sandwich without using anything that I had ever used before. The meat and bread were the only familiar things I could use and I had to find three new things to put on my sandwich.

God was using my sister and my friends to deal with that self-protective place that was rising up. Being among family and friends who love you will help you to put on the new you.

The new you is not actually new at all. Sometimes the obscurity is because of a relationship but sometimes it's just new because so many other falsehoods have hidden you from yourself. It was easy to hide behind my husband and children. I was not interested in who Robyn was, I had to focus on the needs, wants and desires of my family

When God draws the real you to the surface, your attitude towards yourself is very important. Attitude is the determining factor of how smooth or how bumpy the transition will be.

When you feel safe and comfortable about exploring new things about yourself, the true you can't help but be intrigued and it will try to peek through here and there. It's ok, welcome the stirring.

An old photo of me was recently posted on Facebook. I was shocked when I saw it. I am now so far removed from that person I almost didn't recognize myself. I had on baggy clothes and my baseball cap on backward. That was who I was. I always, always, always wore a backward baseball cap. The clothes changed when the cap changed.

There is something that triggers your look that you identify with. Mine was the backward baseball cap. One day, The Lord told me He didn't want me to wear my baseball cap backward anymore. But why? I didn't understand. I liked my cap that way. It seemed harmless. It wasn't hurting anybody. With God, it's either do it or don't do it. In love, of course. There is no gray with Him.

Not wanting to let go of the cap being backward and fighting to keep it was indicative of an internal issue. So I reluctantly let go of it. Without me realizing it, my attire began to change into an attire that complemented the person I was becoming.

Later, He told me that the backward cap affected my attitude. I saw it after I was removed from it for a while. It was hard to see when I was in it. Now if I put a cap on backward just to see (which I did, just to check it out) I can feel the shift in demeanor. I now see what He was saying.

I can remember getting upset about something and out of reflex I grabbed my cap and threw it on backward. That indicated I meant business, it was about to go down. There was a triggering identifier that I needed to let go of. When I did, a lot of pieces began to fall into place.

I told my friend Cathy once that God had me at a particular church to learn how to fight professionally and get out of the street fight mentality. I didn't know why. That just rang true to me.

Years later, it was time for the professional boxing gloves. I liked the street fight. Everything is fair. Anything goes. Not so with a professional fight. A professional fight requires skill, finesse, control, and discipline. It's a whole other level of fight.

The rules in a professional fight definitively establish a winner. A street brawl is a reckless mess of fury flying everywhere and the winner is subject to opinion.

The upset with the lady at the beginning of the book was not about person to person but more so about who I had become being challenged by the situation.

I initially looked at it as person to person. God kept telling me who I used to be was being provoked and who I had become was far stronger.

God has no problem with you knowing the answer. He will tell you the answer Himself. He just wants you to live out the answer as it being a part of who you are, not just what you know. The answer of your true identity is not separate from you; it resides in you and is emerging from hiddenness. Our true identity was hand crafted by God to fit us perfectly.

4 DO THEY KNOW WHO THEY'RE MESSING WITH?

POWER IN REALITY

Love is the most powerful force in the earth. God is love. We're made in His image and after His likeness. Love, real love, has to be understood before it can be fully utilized.

Most people love the way they've been loved or taught to love. My father equated love to correction. He told me he corrected me because he loved me. This is true. God corrects those He loves, but there's more to it.

Consequently, I grew up feeling like if someone didn't correct me, they didn't love me enough to correct the error of my ways. They were waiting for me to fall into a ditch. In actuality, they were loving me the way they were taught love, and the two pictures of love did not speak the same language.

In actuality, love is patient and kind. Love is not jealous, boastful, proud or rude. It does not demand its own way. It is not irritable, and it keeps no record of being wronged. It does not rejoice about injustice but rejoices whenever the truth wins out. Love never gives up, never loses faith, is always hopeful,

and endures through every circumstance. Love lives on forever.
- 1Cor. 13:4-8a (NLT)

God established what love is before any of us arrived on
the scene. Love is a choice. It goes so much further than
affection. If you name the Name of Christ, you are commanded
to love as He loves, not as you were taught, because you have
the ability to. He knows what He's put in us and He requires that
we walk in it.

We are told to love our neighbor as ourself. If you don't or
can't love yourself, how are you going to properly love your
neighbor? Are you patient and kind to yourself? Are you hopeful
to see yourself succeed?

Sometimes we can be our own biggest critics. Do you
refuse to give up on yourself? It can get tough sometimes.
When I feel like giving up on myself, I tell myself, "God believes
in you and so do I. He's confident in what He's put in you, so
trust that it will shine in due time. Keep going, lady, you can do
it!" That's my pep talk to myself. It is based on what He believes
about me because He sees what I don't.

One toughy is love your enemy. I remember when I had to
learn this one. There was a girl at my church operating in
witchcraft. The real deal witchcraft. It had been a part of her
lineage and she operated in it herself. She hadn't fully
relinquished it and she was still trying to be a Christian too. It
was in her family and there were certain things about it that she
identified with and wanted to hold on to.

We were friends and when I was praying for her, God
showed me her heart. He showed me that she wanted to hold
on to some of the things that she had known because she felt
like it made her more powerful than other Christians. I
addressed it with her so that she would know that God's love

for her was bigger than what she was hiding and He wanted her free.

Now that she was exposed, the showdown was on. She took my gesture of love as a challenge. She wasn't backing down and neither was I. There were threats and all sorts of ridiculousness. Jesus destroyed all the works of the enemy, including witchcraft. He said, "I will fight against those who fight against you." He's my fortress, my rock, and my defense. I'm submitted to God, I was not going to give that witchcraft in her any place and her pride would not let her let it go of its power that she had known.

I approached her to help her not to condemn her. The consequences of certain things are already in motion when you've set your heart to do them. Her refusal to fully renounce witchcraft and fully surrender to the Lord had already put consequences in motion; I didn't have to do anything.

You don't have to do anything but let things take their course. What she was doing would take care of itself. I was trying to let her know that you are a slave to who you obey. How can two walk together unless there's agreement? You can walk in religion and witchcraft together but you can not walk with God and witchcraft at the same time. His presence dispels darkness. There is no life and restoration in darkness. There is no fellowship with light and darkness; light dispels darkness.

The Bible says in Matthew 6:22-23 (NKJV)

"The lamp of the body is the eye. If therefore your eye is good, your whole body will be full of light. 23 But if your eye is bad, your whole body will be full of darkness. If therefore the light that is in you is darkness, how great is that darkness!"

Darkened understanding alienates us from the life of God, because of the ignorance that blinds the heart. She could not see and didn't know it. What she had allowed in her life and clung to was darkening her understanding. The only thing that could change that is desire. She had to want to change and then she'd have eyes to see. Her "want to" kept her in darkness.

I've worked in a restaurant with dimmed lighting. When I first started working there, I was in shock. I thought it was too dark and I'd never be able to see to work in there. As the months progressed, I became used to it and it looked "normal". What was happening got my attention when my daughter walked in one day and said to me, "It is always so dark in here. How can you see?"

When you come from the light and step into darkness, the darkness is very evident. The longer you linger in darkness the more your internal light exposure diminishes. This girl's internal lamp had grown dim and her understanding was being darkened by what she allowed in her life as valuable. She did not realize the strength in who she had become in Christ because of what she chose to value over Him.

She was still operating in witchcraft because the old her thought it was more powerful than the new her. She was on a deceptive downward spiral and didn't even know it.

The Bible says people don't change because they love darkness rather than light because light exposes what they're doing. God wants us to love our enemies so they can have an opportunity at experiencing Him and His love for them.

While we were still in our ugliness He loved us, and He wants us to do the same for others because He's alive in us. We have to first be in touch with His love in us to give it away to others.

It goes back to love being a choice. This girl wanted to take me out. The threats were real. He hadn't taught me to fight like a lady yet so it was on; I was ready to throw down. He kept telling me to love her. That was a little hard to grasp in the middle of an all-out war. She wasn't learning a life lesson; I was and it was my life that was the one being used for the lesson. *Love her? Lord, she's trying to kill me. How do you love someone who is truly trying to kill you?*

First of all, your love tank had better be full. Secondly, loving someone does not mean you put down your sword. Loving them is the heart toward them as you swing your sword. Wow. Odd lesson to learn. Remember, love is not how we define it but how He defines it.

The way He taught me this lesson was through the American Civil War. I was homeschooling my children and we were studying the Civil War. Interesting enough, it fit right in with my moment.

When the north and the south were at war with one another, the United States looked very different than they do today. Back then, when they became divided, there were only thirty-four (34) states. The American population was much smaller and it was relatives and business partners who were at war with one another.

They loved the people they were at war with, yet they were in a war nonetheless. They unleashed firebombs on each other. When they ceased fire, whoever had crops left would feed the other side dinner then they'd start back up the next day.

That spoke volumes to me. I'm going to put my sword out there. If my enemy falls on it, that's not my fault. I will love them through their wounds with kindness and patience, but I will not back down or retreat. His love in us is full of power and strength.

One of the other things the Lord showed me about love is that love is kind, love is not nice. Nice will get run over; kind will speak the truth in love, full of grace seasoned with salt, knowing how to answer every man.

The best love lesson I learned was the very hardest ever. This love will produce a strength that you didn't know you had.

There was a situation where I was being accused of something that I didn't do. The Lord told me that I was going to be wrongly accused but not to defend myself. I didn't like that one too much. I can do my own bad, I didn't need any help.

It was important that I didn't defend myself because He needed this person to think he was ok and not to run off. I knew and trusted God as my rock and my defense. I knew He would bring it back around.

I had to meet with some people and they did exactly what He said they'd do and it was not lovely. He kept my mouth silent. In my own self, I would never have let these people speak to me in the manner in which they did. I was savagely brutalized with words and false accusations. If I wanted to, I could prove everything they were saying was wrong, but I kept silent. When I came out of the meeting, I was so verbally abused my entire physical body was in excruciating pain. I had never felt anything like it before in my life. It was the strangest thing to me, that words could cut so deeply that you could feel it in your physical body.

I remember telling the Lord that, as horrible as I felt, it was absolutely nothing in comparison to what He endured for me on the cross. I will never forget what His response to me was. He said, "Can anyone do anything to you now?" He showed me, "No greater love than this than a man lay down his life for his friend." I felt indescribably horrible at the time, but now, being on the other side of it, I can understand love without limits. Love without limits has strength and power.

STRENGTH YOU DIDN'T KNOW YOU HAD

The more love lives in you, on purpose, the greater the strength, and power you walk in. If something gets me upset, I check my love level. I want to walk in such a way that someone else's personal issues do not affect me.

That is strength. Then I am free to give what is working on the inside of me. You can't give what you don't have. You won't have what you don't give attention to. Giving attention to the love within and finding daily outlets for it to shine causes it to grow. No matter what the excuses are, to shrink and draw back causes the love to lay dormant.

People need love. Everyone needs love. Those who reject love the most are the ones who need it the most. When we are confident in ourselves, we are free to love without limitations or attachments, the motives are pure.

When the motives have an agenda behind them and it is not because of who we have become, it's a false love and it will fail. True love that is patient and kind because you are patient and kind has no hidden motives. Learning to love the new you empowers you to love the unlovely in someone else. I've noticed that when I'm concerned for self I don't give out as much love. When I turn my concern towards others, I love freely.

I have a group of great girlfriends, Germaine, Shirell, Molly, Deborah, and Debbie. They have shown me the freedom in loving out of a pure heart. We make a point to get together as often as possible and just enjoy each others company with great belly laughs. We don't expect or require anything from each other. We respect and love each other for all of our unique qualities. They are the greatest at giving love earnestly, selflessly and genuinely. They are a kiss from God. When you can see this in the lives of those you've surrounded yourself with, it will keep you stirred to do the same for others. This is the good kind of seeing yourself in others and desiring to be like them. The love in you is stirred afresh by the love in others.

This love is invigorating. It strengthens you to do more than you thought you had the capacity to do. A good example of this is when two people come together, "fall in love" and they're floating on cloud nine. Life is grand and they both have a spring in their step. There's a euphoric sense of invincibility.

If the relationship starts to decline, the energy drains and heaviness comes. Without realizing it, strength is being drained from each of them. The focus shifts from giving to one another to attention and energy on whatever caused the upset. No one notices the loss of strength.

Knowing that strength comes when love is given away, it's good to nurture and cultivate love in all of our relationships, keeping the power flowing.

Love stirs joy and joy is the secret carrier of strength. Identifying with the euphoric sense of invincibility that comes with freely giving love to another is a part of our spiritual DNA. We are wired this way. It is a very natural way of being. Being aware of it, we can protect it and grow in it.

MUSCLES CAN SPLIT A SHIELD

"Muscles can split a shield and even destroy life itself but only the unseen power of love can open the hearts of man. And until I master this act I will remain no more than a peddler in the marketplace. I will make love my greatest weapon and none on who I call can defend upon its force... my love will melt all hearts liken to the sun whose rays soften the coldest day." I will greet this day with love in my heart. For this is the greatest secret of success in all ventures." - Og Mandino, *The Greatest Salesman In The World.*

This book by Og Mandino is a life changer, an amazing read. It challenges you to become who you know you can be.

One day I had gone to a Costco store with a friend. It was a weekend and we were both enjoying all of the taste samples that were out. We both finished our shopping and were waiting in the very long checkout line. While we were waiting, my friend told me to run back and try a particularly amazing taste sample.

I ran back to grab one but they weren't ready yet. The lady who was making them was very rude. My first response to her rudeness was compassion for her that she was tired and it was probably a long day. So I tried to chit chat a bit with her while I waited. She gave me the ugliest, meanest face ever. With eyebrows raised, I stepped back a bit and waited off to the side.

As I waited, the Lord spoke to me and said, "Love her." Again, my response was one of discontent: *Really, love her? I just want to get my sample and get out of here.* I was not trying to make a new friend or even "make her day". She had obviously already ruined it herself with her bad attitude I thought.

(Side note: If you're a little discontent about how much I've said about what God has spoken to me, I'm only communicating it how I've lived it. He is very real to me. If I were speaking about what my husband or a friend had said to me over the years to teach me valuable life lessons, I would reference them often, just the same.)

Well, I knew what to do, I just didn't want to. Remember, love is a choice. Her upset did not trigger love in me, it made me want to walk away and leave her in her ugliness.

I always want to please Papa God more than I want my own way, so I stirred up love within myself and stepped back into her unwelcoming circle. I decided to ignore her rudeness and respond as though she was really enjoying my conversation.

I had to watch myself not to get joy out of being a nuisance to her. That was not my intent but that's what was happening. Finding joy in her upset is not love and it would not have yielded the desired results. She remained stone-faced as I made small talk and spoke as kindly as I could.

When the tasty treats came out of the oven, people swarmed the table instantaneously. I immediately interrupted the stampede and made all of the hunger vultures stop and say thank you to her. I said something like, "You could at least say thank you. She's had a long day and kindness is always appreciated." The people slowed down and mumbled thank yous as they walked away.

Amazing results! Her cold, hard expression instantly melted away to a soft, tender smile. Who would have thought, simple words and acts of love could have such dramatic results in just moments?

That was an example of letting the love in me outshine the upset in her. My secret weapon of love opened her heart and melted away the coldness.

LETTING LOVE LIVE

Practicing love on purpose causes the love to live and to thrive within us. I get more joy out of deliberate acts of love as opposed to love as a defense to someone else's hard-heartedness. Either way is truly a win-win situation. Loving on purpose takes on the identity of who we were created to be.

The power of love creates a shield around us that gives us immunity to the upsets of life. Life is life. There will be ups, downs, and arounds. How we respond to them determines the quality of life that we will have. Having an intentional love life puts the controls back in your hands.

How many people like control freaks? I sure don't. I've encountered my share of them. I must have a hidden control freak magnet on me somewhere.

I always found it difficult to work alongside that type of personality because everything you say they take the exact opposite way, deliberately. Whether it's right or wrong, it didn't matter then they'd have the craziest excuse as to why it didn't work. I'll tell you why it didn't work, it didn't make sense to begin with; you just wanted your way. It's irritating to me because they care more about controlling the situation than what's best for the situation.

I've known very stealthy controllers. The way you smoke them out is to never let them see you sweat. When they cannot elicit a reaction out of you, they usually become perturbed and get pushy. Just keep calm; that means you're winning.

I once worked for an organization that taught us to be master of our emotions. In mastering your emotions, you'll master the emotional environment around you. Someone else can get upset but your internal environment remains fixed, which empowers you to bring stability to those around you.

My remedy is to diffuse love. Operating in patience and kindness but refusing to play their game works masterfully. Again, your love tank must be full in order to do this. If it's not, they win because you're being squeezed by their tactics for their sheer pleasure, nothing more. True love never fails. It's doable, you just have to practice it till it becomes who you are; till you identify with love. Love will empower you to walk unencumbered by the heaviness in the lives of others.

5 WHY ME?

KNOWING WHAT THE ENEMY IS AFTER

A thief steals when you're not looking. If you know what he came to steal, you know how to protect it from being taken. There's an enemy who wants your strength. This enemy wants to incapacitate you and take you out of the game. He wants to win.

In any competitive game, strength is necessary for winning. Mental, physical or spiritual; whatever is being tried is that which needs the strength.

Love and strength go hand in hand. It is in our spiritual DNA to have joy in walking out love. Joy is the fire of strength.

As I mentioned earlier, I homeschooled all three of my children. One day, my son Joel was having a challenge with one of the math problems he had to do. This was very upsetting to him because he was excellent at math. The longer he spent on the problem the more frustrated he became because he knew he should know how to do it.

After being frustrated and upset for a while, he soon became disheartened. When he asked for my help, I looked at his countenance and realized I could just show him how to get the right answer or I could make this a life lesson that would show him how to get the right answer plus teach him how to master his emotions, where they worked for him and not against him.

When you're emotionally drained, you can't think as well as when your emotions are high and soaring. An essential key to living strong and powerful is to know how to be master of your emotions. When your emotions are on the decline, you have to have a game plan in place to maintain your emotional footing.

I made him stand up from the table, jump up and down and laugh on purpose. Given his present state of upset, you know that went over really well. It didn't matter, my answer wasn't what he was looking for, but it was my answer.

So, reluctantly, he stood up, bounced his shoulders around (not jumping yet) and coughed out chomped up bits of laughter. We kept going till he was actually jump, jump, jumping around and truly laughing from his gut. He was starting to have fun with this, but I had to cut the party short and get him back to his school work.

When he sat back down, I told him to take a deep breath, look at the problem again and think through it one more time; if he didn't get it and still needed my help then I'd show him how to do it.

Well, what do you know? He saw something he didn't see before, got the answer and plowed through the rest of his work, all on his own. That simple, little exercise helped him to regain his mental strength that had been fatigued through despair.

If I can't get something that I know I should know, I will start laughing. If I need strength to endure, I'll start laughing. I will deliberately stir joy so that my heart may be continuously anchored in strength, which, in turn, yields peace. The environment that we draw from is the environment of our hearts. We have to diligently protect our hearts.

I remember getting a phone call one day from someone I was dreading to speak to. The phone rang and as I cringed when I went to answer it, my friend, who was with me at the time, stopped me real quickly and told me to wait—then she pressed the end button on my phone that sent the caller to voicemail.

What a novel idea. I'm sure most of you already know to do that, but my personality type is a bit different. If I don't answer, I'm saying I'm not available. Well, that's not true. I'm right here and I can answer the phone. One little statement from my insightful friend changed everything. She said to me, "Just because someone wants your attention doesn't mean you have to answer right then. You answer them when you're ready, on your time, not theirs. No, you're not available for them right now."

That gave me time to position my heart for the emotions that best suited me and the situation, stress-free, also from a place of strength and peace.

If I let situations stirred by others dictate my emotions, then my heart and emotions are subject to the ups and downs of others. Choosing to be master of my emotions keeps me at the helm of my own ship and not subject to the life storms of others.

Emotions have power. What you do with your power-packed emotions is what matters. They can steer your life to greatness or destruction, but it's you who decides what direction they will take.

I had an acquaintance that had gotten injured in a relationship. The woman just totally took advantage of him. He took the upset from that relationship and wrote a book. He made money off of her foolishness. Brilliant.

Situations can draw out your strength; but it's your perspective that determines who will win, you or them.

YOU HAVE TO KNOW WHAT'S VALUABLE TO PROTECT WHAT'S VALUABLE

The guards stationed around Buckingham Palace are there for a reason. They are not castle props for tourists. They are Britain's finest, militarily trained soldiers. These sentries are stationed to protect access to the palace and the queen. The queen and her family are Britain's most valuable assets. They govern the entire country of Great Britain. A nation of people is dependent upon them and the decisions that they make on behalf of their country.

Our heart is one of the most valuable assets that we have. With all diligence, it is to be guarded. Out of our hearts flow the issues of our lives. The heart is the seat of our emotions, from whence our choices and decisions stem. If we are not trained to steward our emotions with excellence, they will rule our choices and decisions out of sheer dominance.

Emotions can have an intensified trajectory, either up or down, if not properly governed and balanced. Excitement can send you soaring into elation while depression can send you plummeting into despair.

Reasonings of the heart bring either balance or imbalance to emotions that spark action. Internal reasonings of the heart are the justifiers for one's emotional temperament.

In reference to the story at the beginning of the book, the reasonings in my heart of a justifiable brawl were what enhanced and fortified my emotions. My emotions flared up and they needed an excuse to respond. Justification was the inner agreement that my actions needed to respond.

If I did not have inner boundaries in place as guards over my heart, a reflexive emotional response with justifiable agreement would have resulted in a really good knock-down-drag-out fist fight. My emotions went soaring and my cultural reasoning gave justification for the desired result—beat her down.

In my reestablished walk with the Lord, I learned to set boundaries for myself. Inner boundaries. Many people set external boundaries, which are great, but our actions begin within. External boundaries are only as strong as the inner boundaries that align with them.

Inner boundaries deal with the root issue of things. Why do we want or desire that which is not healthy for us? If the desire of the thing is not dealt with, shifting and moving things out of external reach is only temporal.

There was a time in my life when I did some things that you could not have convinced me early on that I would ever do. During that time, I had a good, long talk with God and told Him I was scared of me.

It was then that I asked Him to show me how to deal with myself. At that point, I didn't know if there was anything that I wouldn't do. He started showing me how to set inner boundaries that fortified me in who He created me to be, instead of boundaries made up of rules and regulations that say, "don't do this and don't do that".

God began to show me, who I fear and who I do not fear, what I find joy in and what I do not find joy in, what I love and what I hate is valuable and necessary. He reoriented my perspective.

Fear, joy, love and hate are emotions that are gatekeepers of the heart. When they're in proper order and balance we have a healthy soul. Out of order, they are the root cause of the disarrays of life.

There is a famous comedian (who shall remain nameless) who many people find extremely funny. Although he is definitely humorous, his words and analogies propagate death and destruction.

This gentleman (I say very loosely) does not understand the power of his words. I would say he does, from the knowledge that what he says incites laughter, but he is ignorant of the fact that death and life are in the power of his words. If he were aware of the true end result of his words, he'd use them for life and liberty.

As we saw earlier in the example of my son and his school work, there's strength in joy. A component of love and joy is to cause one's heart to open up. If you remember the lady at Costco, love caused her heart to soften and open up.

The enemy of mankind truly has been stripped of all his power and authority. The Bible says that Jesus put the enemy's defeat on open display in His triumph over him. The issue is the enemy's attempt to control these four emotions of the heart of man. In doing so, he uses man as a puppet.

As the queen and Buckingham Palace are Britain's most valuable assets, your heart, and your brain are two of the most valuable assets that you have in life. They work hand-in-hand. With all diligence, we are to guard them.

EQUIPPED TO DO AND TO BE

With a strong heart and vigilant mind, we are well equipped to walk in the image and likeness of God as we were created. Anything less, we're cheating ourselves.

All that we were created and designed to be is within us. When we realize it's within and not without, it will be a lot easier to press into the greatness that's readily available.

Looking outside of ourselves says that we do not have what it takes and we are reliant upon someone or something to empower us to become. People and things are contributors to living out all that we are but the core of our identity is within. External things are accessories and enhancements. When we draw from within to pour into the lives and needs of others, we are causing the growth and maturity of the nature of God in us to shine forth our reflection of His goodness, which we already possess from being made in His image and likeness. It's really easy to do when we shift perspective.

Generosity from a heart of love and joy is an intricate part of the amalgamation of our true identity. Everything about God is good. As we pour out love and joy into the lives and hearts of others, without any requirements or strings attached, we are creating moments for others to taste and see that He is good. Giving generously has always been a heart opener. We have the liberty to not only to give generously but creatively.

Using creativity in our generosity is equivalent to the refractions of light shining forth from a diamond, brilliant and striking in luster.

I remember being invited to an after Christmas gift exchange. My friend Cathy came up with the brilliant idea to invite our friends over for a gift auction party. Instead of re-gifting the Christmas gifts we didn't want later on throughout the year, we'd auction them off to each other and give the proceeds to a worthy cause. I thought, *Wow, that's a great idea. How beautiful is that?*

Everyone was excited about the idea and brought things that were great gifts but they just didn't want them. The energy of the room was high from the joy of giving. After the auction was complete, we raised a nice amount to give to "a worthy cause". At the end, I found out that I was the "worthy cause"!

I was in tears! Cathy and all of our friends did this for me. Some were just friends of hers who I didn't even know. They came just to be a part of the love of giving. Cathy felt that widows are not taken care of in the church as they should be and she did what she knew to do. I have countless stories of her creative style of love and generosity.

Cathy is a prime example of using creativity, love and joy to express the goodness of God. There is a fulfillment in exploring generosity through the eyes of creativity. It's the very heart of God that He deposited within each one of us. Creativity in giving generously is God's thumbprint on our lives. It causes the entire environment of the heart to emanate love and strength.

FINDING ME AND LOVE ME

Creativity is the hidden mirror of self. It speaks volumes about who you are and what you feel. What you feel is the voice and expression of your emotions. Creativity gives voice to yourself with the impact of your feelings.

Emotions and feelings can be seen and felt through various artistic pieces such as music, dance and fine art in multiple mediums.

I shared earlier that as a child I thought I didn't have any "talent" because the artist had not yet emerged. We all have a left and right brain hemisphere, the right side being the creative side and the left side being the logical side. If we were only logical without any creativity, we would not have both sides; we'd only have the one.

We're all creative. Some have just tapped into it more so than others. When we're reasoning with a situation our creative thinking usually has its own thought process that's not as clearly at the forefront as conscious logical thought is when trying to "solve a problem". To get a "creative" solution, we have to shift out of logical thinking.

Artists often reference their "feelings" as the major directive influence in their work. There is definitely a harmony between both sides of the brain that is essential to realizing your true self.

Only acknowledging one and not the other is crippling to the true you. It is said that we only use ten percent of our brain. Acknowledgment that there is more to explore is a great starting point.

If you are prone to the logical side, there are exercises that you can do to activate creativity. If you favor the creative side, exploring the logical side should not be a foreign concept.

Fear of one side or the other because of unfamiliarity or lack of experience is usually the culprit for not pursuing the least favored hemisphere of the brain. Whichever side we do favor most is a part of who you are and your uniqueness. How we view someone else's gifting or strength is not the measuring rod for who we are or our value.

It's very easy to assess what is valued and honored in one's life. Simply chronicle the hours of your day in the form of a plus and minus accounting spreadsheet. Start with twenty-four hours and minus out each activity of the day, hour by hour, minute by minute. Categorize your time into types of activities and calculate your weekly categories and, after thirty days, see where the majority of your time is spent.

You "spend" time on what is most valuable to you. For most, it's our work. That's also easy. Work is valuable because of its necessity. What really needs to be looked at is our ancillary and discretionary time. Is the prep and support weighted down with "want tos" instead of sheer necessities? Our discretionary time speaks volumes about what we truly value. This is the time in which we do as we choose without anyone telling us what to do. This is where "I'm the boss of me."

This reminds me of when I went on a trip out of town about a year ago. My children, who are no longer little children anymore, they're young adults, were left at home to fend for themselves. My youngest was nineteen at the time. I was only going to be gone for three to four days and they could surely hold down the fort for that length of time.

I arrived back home from my trip and the house looked like it had been "thrown" back together. I didn't say anything; I just kind of smirked on the inside because I knew what had happened. I wasn't going to say anything to anyone, I was just going to let it seem as though all was well and they'd kept everything tidy and in order while I was gone.

A few days later, Aryel, my youngest, came to me and said, "Mom, after two days we came home and the house was a mess, we looked at each other and said, 'We need Mom.'" I just laughed because I knew what had happened. When it was time for me to come home, they tried their best to recover from no one having to tell them to pick up after themselves. They were their own boss; they could do what they wanted.

Their discretionary time was at the forefront. All of their "like tos" were speaking loud and clear. Pizza boxes everywhere. Open two-liter bottles of soda. Watching Netflix all night. Dirty dishes in the living room. Clothes all over the floor. They were the boss of themselves, and their "want tos" were taking over.

When our "want tos" take over our discretionary time without proper restraint or discipline they become consumers. When properly trained and exercised, they can be one of our greatest assets. Our wants and desires are trainable because they're appetite driven.

When we choose to take responsibility for our wants and desires, down to the fine details of our discretionary time, we can hone a life of creative productivity.

People look at me shocked when I first tell them that I drink as much as I want to and I smoke as much as I want to. They look at me all wide eyed. I then smile and say, "I just don't want to." It's not because I'm a Christian that I don't smoke or drink, it's because I truly don't want to. I have no appetite for it. I use to do both but not anymore. I've chosen a better quality of life from who I've become. Appetites are trainable.

I'm a life coach with a few specialties. I once helped someone to stop smoking who had tried so many things and couldn't quit. I first had to address her want tos. That's what really drives the appetites on various levels.

Our "want tos" speak volumes about who we are. They so very often go unchecked because they're so familiar we don't realize the value they carry in truly getting to know ourselves.

I remember seeing the movie "The Runaway Bride". What was interesting about that movie was that she truly did not have her own identity. She'd assume the identity, likes and dislikes of her fiancé, all the way down to the types and style of food she ate.

I found that very puzzling in that she was so numb to her own self that she didn't recognize that she changed her "favorite breakfast" to reflect that of each new fiancé. Her identity was found in who she was in a relationship with.

In the business of life, it's easy to assume what you like and don't like without really giving yourself the time and respect to actually explore your true likes and dislikes. So it becomes easy to take on the likes and dislikes of others and lose ourselves in the process.

It's hard to genuinely love someone you don't spend quality time with, that includes yourself. Having still, quiet, me time is essential. My suggestion would be to go to a new remote place where you can sit in undisturbed stillness. Do not make requirements of self; just allow self to enjoy self's company.

A solitary beach day, park day or any quiet getaway place is a great start to begin exploring who self is and what self's actual likes and dislikes are. If you're one of those people who are so overwhelmed with the inter-workings of life, it's a good possibility self is like unto a distant relative. This process may take some getting used to, again like sitting down with a distant relative that you may struggle to make conversation with.

After repetitive quiet time with self, introduce into your self-time something creative. Journaling is a good place to begin or a blank piece of paper and three colors of acrylic paint and a paint brush. Begin simple and unimposing. Give self the liberty to be expressive without any critique, correction or judgment. Be that safe place for yourself that you would expect or like to receive from others.

Finding self or discovering more about self can take time, but you're well worth it. Sometimes we treat ourselves like the little kid wanting their parent's attention but the parent is too engrossed in their own thing to give the child their full, undivided attention. So the child gets the brush off, ignored or divided attention. This, in and of itself, would make the child feel like they're not valuable, or unworthy of attention. Far too many have grown up this way.

We have to stop and give attention to ourselves—full, undivided attention—and be generous and consistent. When this is done for a child, it tells them that they matter and what they have to say is important. Self-time full of attention to the inner heart and voice of self, says to one's self that you're important, valuable and treasured.

I'm all for spa pampering but that's not the same as turning inward and saying to self, "You matter. Your thoughts matter. Your feelings matter. I want to hear what you have to say, what you feel and why you feel that way. I believe what you have to say is important. I love you and believe in you." I believe that when we take the time to honor the person of self in such a way that speaks love to who we are as a person, we can easily recognize how valuable we are without trying to win the approval of others.

Far too often approval and validation are sought from others because there is a negative perception of self that needs to be convinced otherwise. People engage in negative self-talk all the time, will but will look to others to speak the good talk to them and about them.

I power talk myself quite often. It's really funny how that came about. One time, my late husband David and I were headed home from a little mini road trip. I had asked him to do something that he hadn't done. He deliberately hadn't done it because that was his way of getting back at me when he was angry at me. So I started talking to myself in the third person as if I was a southern, black grandma, accent and all. "Baby, you knows I'm prayns fa ya. Now, don't chu let none of dats make you upset." I went on and on and on and on and on for the last hour of the ride home. The first few minutes, he just shook his head at me. After about twenty minutes into it, he began to look a little concerned for me 'cause he thought I would have let up by then. I didn't, I kept going. The more I went on the funnier it got, and the funnier it got the more I went on. I was on a roll and couldn't stop. I did that for a whole hour, on and on and on.

What was happening was I was beginning to feel the love and encouragement. It was partly funny because I was making it up as I went along and then I was beginning to feel the strength from the joy in it. What could have turned into a very bad argument, leaving me feeling hurt from the situation, turned out to be a very valuable lesson.

I had never thought to encourage myself for any extended length of time. Maybe a few words muttered here and there, like, "Come on, Robyn, you can do it," or "I can do this. Just keep pushing," but that was about it. Never any long monologue like that. When I was done, I felt encouraged, strengthened and empowered. It was okay that he hadn't done what I asked; it was all going to work out anyway.

Someone once said, "It's ok to talk to yourself as long as you don't answer yourself." Hmmmm. My thought on that statement is you should answer yourself so that you can make the conversation conclusive.

When you encourage yourself on purpose, you begin to take control over the random thoughts of doubt and discouragement that sometimes seem to surface out of nowhere. Our mental ground is very valuable space. We must enforce our ownership of it by maintaining a secure guard over it.

6 GOD IS JUST

GOD'S WISDOM

Do not take revenge, my dear friends, but leave room for God's wrath, for it is written: "It is mine to avenge; I will repay," says the Lord. On the contrary: "If your enemy is hungry, feed him; if he is thirsty, give him something to drink. In doing this, you will heap burning coals on his head." Romans 12:19-20

God's judgments are just. There is no one who loves greater or deeper than God. There is no one who understands the depth and power of love more than God does. There's a novel written by William P. Young called *The Shack*. The book was written to explain to his children about a tragedy that happened to his niece. It has been a high controversial book in many Christian circles. After getting past my scrutiny with extremely high reservations, I found it to be one of the most phenomenal books I have ever read. God's love made evident in this book is profound.

In his book, Mr. Young speaks about the judgment of God and how we judge God and judge others through a perceived righteous stance that we carry. It is amazing and very liberating. I will not spoil it for you if you decide to get a copy of it. It succinctly and clearly dismantles any stance one could ever make to take justice out of God's hands and place it into our own hands.

In any given situation, God always wants us to be anchored in love. He tells us to be angry but don't sin. He knows that situations can cause our emotions to soar. He gave us the emotions; He knows what they're capable of. In His wisdom, He tells us the right answer but lets us keep our freedom to choose either right or wrong.

There was a time when the Lord had me praying for a very prominent Christian leader, who, honestly speaking, I didn't want to pray for. I felt like he was doing something wrong purposefully and wondered why I was spending my prayer time praying for him when he obviously wanted to have his own way.

God let me know very clearly that my prayers were not to "make" him make the right choice, but it was for him to have a door of grace and mercies remaining open for him to have available when he changed his heart and mind. God will not allow any of us to be tempted beyond what we're able, but also, make a way of escape for us. He told me to pray for him like I would want someone praying for my own personal brother.

That really changed my heart about praying for people when "I felt like" they didn't "deserve" my prayers. How self-righteous is that? That was so horrible for me to think that way, but when God shows you, you, He does it in such love, but undeniable truth. I was judging this man's worthiness of my prayers! Yuk! How disgusting! Thank you, Lord, for loving me in my ugliness!

God may have us sometimes doing something for someone that we "feel" is "unfair". Self-righteousness will try to judge the situation and say, "Surely, God, you've given them plenty enough love and grace." Who are we to put a barometer on God's long suffering?

At the start of this book, when I was dealing with the woman I wanted to go toe-to-toe with, I had plenty of self-righteous justification because she started it and I hadn't done anything to provoke it.

God kept talking to me about my attitude and why I was feeling the way that I was. Really, He was saying, "Why are you letting that situation push you out of the love that I've placed in your heart?"

Self-righteousness will taint your perspective. The love of God does not reside in self-righteousness, love of self, does. Ouch. Humility allows His love to reign in our hearts.

God is extremely patient but there is a point when He will allow someone to have their own way. He'll remove Himself and allow the circumstances to take their course. I call it *giving someone enough rope to hang themselves*. He has spoken, "There is a way that seems right to a man but its end is the way of death." (Prov. 14:12, 16:25)

I've told the Lord plenty of times, in prayer, *DO NOT let me have my own way!* I have enough sense to know that, no matter what I think, He sees far beyond what I see and know. His way is ALWAYS better than my own.

When your heart trusts in the Lord, you become aware that His wisdom far surpasses your own. It's just not in the selfish nature of man to think that God sees and knows more than self. You can't trust both yourself and God simultaneously, you have to choose one. Trust gives voice to the decision you make.

A double-minded person is unstable in all of his ways. To trust God in all of our ways, even the ones we think we understand, empowers Him on the throne of our hearts.

Self-centeredness is all about our greatness, not our weakness, so, of course, that greatness is seen above and beyond what it really is because it's the fruit of pride. Pride distorts vision. Humility removes the plank out of your own eye so that you can see clearly to help others. Love and humility are the filters of God's wisdom.

GOD'S WAY

Trusting God begins with a choice. The choice is to let pride die that humility can live. Humility gives place for the heart to have ears to hear. Pride blinds the eyes. It's a false guard. We are not to think of ourselves more highly than we ought. Pride is a distorted view of self.

How can God's vindication have its way when pride, all the while, is standing in the way, saying, "I got this"? Pride is a false wall of protection. It has nothing but a misconstrued perception of justice and ability. Pride is selfish and has nothing but self's own intentions at heart. There is no true justice in pride.

A heart of humility gives us ears to hear; how we hear determines what we see and what we see equals what we get. To hear clearly the ways of God we have to relinquish the god of self. That can be a hard one to dethrone, particularly for those of us who've been trained all of our lives to trust no one but self, be self-sufficient, be independent. Dethroning the god of self is doable, it begins with a willing heart.

Although many have grown up with the instinct to trust no one but self, all along the way, God has placed "Trust Me" signs along the path of our lives. His light is within every person who enters the earth.

There is a natural affinity in man to be drawn to the light. When my oldest daughter was in my womb, my husband would put a lamp on different sides of my stomach. As he moved the light around, she would move to wherever the light was.

Again, we're made in His image. He's configured in each person's DNA a thread of Himself. He has left His fingerprint on mankind and creation.

There's a gentleman by the name of Dr. Hugh Ross. He has written a book called *The Fingerprint of God*. He's an astrophysicist. This man is absolutely brilliant. The book is written in such a way that anyone that is not strong in physics or the sciences can understand and enjoy the book, yet it's so intelligently written it's intriguing for anyone who has a love and appreciation for the sciences. It's an absolutely fascinating book on how you can see the fingerprint of God on all of His creation. Simply amazing.

God's fingerprints are on each of our lives. We are already marked for greatness. The question is will we turn our conscious heart towards His greatness within us for activation?

It is within each of us to trust God and to seek out His way of doing things; His way as He, Himself, being God and not us. The problem comes when we are gods unto ourselves. Once we get self off of the throne of our own hearts then we can hear God when He speaks. His way becomes clear.

It's called surrender. I can't do it all and I'm not called to do it all nor be it all. Let God be God. He's God all by Himself.

Although His ways are higher than our ways and His thoughts are higher than our thoughts, it is His heart to make

His ways known to us. How can two walk together unless they are agreed? It's His desire and His design for us to know the thoughts and ways of His heart, but only He can reveal it to us and only we can relinquish our heart unto Him for access.

As we draw near to Him, He draws near to us. We can live our lives inside of Him; to move and live and have our very being. This empowers us to see life from His perspective, His way. His wisdom, His strength and His heart will arise within us.

In it all, His concern is for our hearts. He tells us to hold our peace and let Him fight our battles. Maintaining a heart of peace, knowing that His justice shall prevail, keeps us in place of grace and strength. There's renewed strength in waiting on God. It's a very stabilizing and anchoring place to reside.

It requires greater strength to hold your peace in a difficult place than to lose your cool because you feel justified in the moment; we're right and they're wrong. Holding your peace seems unfair. Self-justification says, "I have a right to..."

It takes greater fortitude to govern your heart with a resolve of peace. An emotion-driven person is subject to the conditions of their environment controlled by the whims of others.

> He who is slow to anger is better than the mighty,
> And he who rules his spirit than he who takes a city.
> Proverbs 16:32 (NKJV Bible)

God always wants us on the winning side. He spoke everything into existence and upholds everything by the power of His Word. He knows what the course of action His Words that have already been spoken will take. That is why He can say even though in your own mind it may seem right, it will end in death.

Proverbs, the book of wisdom, says this twice, the exact same way in two different verses:

> "There is a way that seems right to a man,
> But its end is the way of death."
> Proverbs 14:12, 16:25 (NKJV Bible)

Today it's the common opinion of many ("common" and "many" is a warning sign in-and-of itself) that you should do what you "feel" is right (or seems right) as long as it makes you happy. I ask you, since when does the clay know what is capable of making it happy? He's the potter, we're the clay. He knows how He's wired the clay for joy and happiness.

When we see the responsiveness of others to a situation and equate that with happiness, it doesn't mean that they're actually happy, nor does it mean that what they're doing has brought true joy.

A drunken person cannot tell you that they're happy because they're unconscious to the true stimuli of happiness; they're inebriated. Alcoholics Anonymous (AA) is filled with millions of people all over the world who have discovered that a drunken stupor does not bring happiness. Yet, in their moments of drunkenness, they're laughing and appearing to be "having a good time", all-the-while, their hearts are aching deep down inside.

Narcotics Anonymous (NA) and Sex Addicts Anonymous (SAA) have also discovered that these falsified forms of happiness are addictive but empty; there is no joy or happiness to be found there. These groups are an allegiance of multitudes upon multitudes grappling to salvage what's left of their lives as a result of trying to find happiness in all the wrong places.

There are also "many" who try to find happiness in purchasing things, ultimately find them empty and unfulfilling, so they have to go and buy the next latest and greatest purse, shoes, dress, car, boat, house, island, etc. Our ways of doing things, apart from Him, are oftentimes futile and empty. Sin has pleasure for a season. No one is denying the legitimacy of the pleasure to be had. What is not widely advertised in the fun-in-the-sun pleasures of sin are the consequences that are reaped in the other three seasons of life.

Our pathways of both happiness and justice come from the same heart where either true or false identity reside. Only the maker of a thing can define its purpose and the intricate characteristics of strength and wisdom that it holds.

It is only God Himself who can show us our true selves. He knows where to find the joys of life on Earth. His ways bring joy, peace, and justice.

GOD'S WIN

I remember my children having fusses when they were little. All three of them would come running to me, to tell me "their side" of the story. All three felt like they were "right" and the other person was wrong and needed disciplining.

By the time my children had gotten to me, they had concluded the matter and determined the justice for me to carry out. Sometimes we do that with God. I know for myself, oftentimes, I have come to Him with a problem and have already concluded the matter; I just want Him to confirm that I was right and let me know what I've deemed "fair" to do about the situation is the correct route to take. Again, I'm looking for His stamp of approval to validate my justification that was concluded from a heart of selfishness.

As I stated at the beginning of the book, when I went to God about the person I was having a problem with, I wanted Him to confirm that I was right and she was wrong, and to please be ok with me vindicating myself. When we've died to self, the question to God becomes, "What's the real issue of this situation and how do I best handle it in Your wisdom, love and grace?"

As a parent of three children, I see that all three of them have very different personalities. They sometimes, truly, could not see eye to eye. No matter how it was explained to them it, was difficult for them to understand why one or the other did a certain thing.

We may not always understand each person we encounter, no matter how hard we try, but suffice to say, peace will reign when we're ok to agree to disagree with respect for the other person. Trouble ensues when either party is selfish and insists on, their own way [as children often do].

Just because someone doesn't see something the way we see it does not mean there has to be a war over whatever the issue is. Conflict and war come into play when neither side will yield to the other; it is then that war ensues for dominance.

My children learned very quickly, the winner in any upset was not who was right or wrong but the one who first pursued peace. That was the winner of the argument. That was the one who was in the right. This person is the one who now has an ear to hear because they've chosen peace over pride that insists on its own way. Pride does not have an ear to hear. It stunts your inner growth. The peacemaker wins because they have squashed pride and chose peace. The one who pursues peace eliminates strife, confusion, and every evil work.

God tells us that with all that is within us to pursue peace. Maintaining peace is truly inner dominance. A true lady (or gentleman) fights from a place of victory. God's peace maintains a soft heart, where love and kindness flow.

There are some who are skilled at a great poker face, their words are smoother than butter but they have war in their hearts. It's like their words are softer than oil, yet they were drawn swords. One who can choose to maintain a soft heart in the midst of anger and upset has true dominance and strength.

The trained poker face, or the skilled corporate person with all the right answers, has hidden motives of the heart. The person who is skilled at maintaining a heart of peace can be a third party to the upset, control the environment with peace and find wisdom for a solution that is best for the whole.

Selfish anger is just that, selfish and self-seeking. There is no resolve for the whole. It's all about self. Even though God's immense love for us wants the absolute best for us in every situation, in His infinite wisdom, He knows how to choose the best for us as well as the best for the whole.

God's first priority is our hearts, the question being is our heart in the right place? When I taught my children to pursue peace first, what that really did was teach them that their heart was the first priority in the situation and then they'd have the right perspective to hear and see what was going on.

Jesus tells us to judge righteously. A scripture that is often misquoted says to take the plank out of your own eye that you may see to take the speck out of your brother's eye. It doesn't *just* say to take the plank out of your own eye (how it's often misquoted). It doesn't say you're not to judge. What it is saying is to deal with yourself first that you may see *how* to judge rightly.

I've learned to quickly forgive, even in the very moment of an upset, forgive. When you do it quickly, as a lifestyle or habit, the upset doesn't have time to take root and have to be dealt with later.

Unforgiveness can definitely be a plank in one's eye. When we can't see past the hurt, pain or injustice, we become offended and give place to self-righteousness. Offense is a hidden killer. John Bevere has written an excellent must-read book on offense, entitled *The Bait of Satan*. Life changer!

As a good Father, God wants us to be able to judge things rightly out of love, compassion, and wisdom. It is His truth that is the standard by which we are to judge.

Humility lets us see ourselves from God's perspective. Not more highly than we ought to, but from a place that understands all that we are and all that we are not is because of Who He is and what He has done for us.

No matter how hard we've worked on something, it's all about what we've done with what He gave us. It's called stewardship. We are responsible for stewarding with excellence the gifts and talents that came from Him. We will all give account to Him for what we've done with them.

Likewise, we are held accountable for stewarding our hearts with excellence, as well. In the manner that we judge others, we will be judged. Keeping a heart of love and that is free from unforgiveness gives us eyes to see rightly to assess a situation for the greater good.

When I walked through learning the lesson of love that lays down one's life for his friend that I mentioned in chapter four, there was a situation with that same lady a week or so later.

She and I were social friends prior to having that situation. We were sitting next to each other in church. Right after worship, when everyone was getting ready to sit down, she passed me an open-paged invitation to a party then asked me to pass it to someone else! Out of discretion, one would have folded it in half but, no, she wanted me to see it. Ordinarily, I would have been invited, but now I wasn't and, on top of it, she handed it to me to pass it on to someone else.

At this point, I just looked at her and shook my head out of pity for her. My thoughts were, *You are so petty, you're definitely the one with the problem.* Then the defensive, self-consolation, judgment kicked in: *I don't care, you WILL reap what you sow!*

In that very moment, God said to me, "Ask Me to show her mercy." Now, you know I was like, "WHAT? Ask YOU to show her MERCY? Lord, really!"

He was not going for any of that. He said, "Either do or don't do it." All of this happened in a nanosecond. He wasn't giving me the option of a discussion, it was either do it or don't do it.

Look, I know my Papa; I did it! It wasn't that it was something detrimental; it was something He was giving me the option of doing out of His arsenal of wisdom. I've learned that anything He suggests is the wiser choice. He was giving me a moment to let self die that the greater part of Him in me may live.

The very moment I did it, I felt like King Ahasuerus extending his scepter to Queen Esther. He extended mercy to her when she came into his courts to see him without being summoned because she could have lost her life. (See the account in Esther 4:11, 5:2) That was just a taste of what He does for us. In that moment, I got to sit in His seat. God judges righteously. There is power and strength in asking God to extend mercy to someone who very well deserves the judgment of reaping what they've sown.

In situations like this, God does not have to pronounce judgment on anyone. When people say that God's judgment has hit in places of disasters, I'm not of that school of thought. The reason is sin has its own consequences; God doesn't have to "send disaster" to pass judgment, yet He can. The elements of one's actions are what sets judgment in motion (like unto the law of gravity, it exists without our permission). It's the spiritual cause and effect with entropy at the helm.

The law of gravity says what goes up must come down; it is a natural law that was set in motion upon creation of the earth and its atmosphere. No one can change it no matter how much they want to disagree with it; it is what it is without anyone's agreement or disagreement. You either learn to work with it and excel or work against it, which will prove detrimental.

We, as people, will reap what we've sown in everything we do. It is not in some things you do and some things you don't. God is not mocked, whatsoever a man sows that shall he also reap. God has already spoken it and there's nothing anyone can do about it; everyone will give account of themselves and their words (which is a product of our hearts) good or bad.

He does give us the right to choose but we do not get to choose the consequences of our choices. He has said, "I've placed before you, death and life; choose life that you and your seed may live." How brilliant is He? He identifies what is in operation in the atmosphere around us and then tells us the answer!

Everything we do is a part of the spiritual and natural atmosphere of the earth that God set in place before it was inhabited by man. He knows what path will bring healthy living and what path will bring destruction. He knows all that is going on around us that we don't yet know and are still discovering.

God's mercy supersedes everything. When He asked me to ask Him to extend mercy to that person, it taught me so much. I will oftentimes either show mercy when someone definitely does not deserve it or ask Papa God to show them mercy. I've discovered that if I want mercy extended to me, I want to extend it to others. Even though His mercies are new every morning, I want to sow mercy whenever I have the opportunity and exercise righteous judgment, as a responsibility afforded to me as a child of God.

God's win is that we walk like He walks, love like He loves and judge like He'd judge. Our heart alignment with His heart helps us to walk in righteous judgment of our own life situations. It's not difficult, it's just a choice and He's already set us up for the win. Humility of heart is what postures our heart to win.

7 KNOW WHERE TRUE POWER LIES

POWER BEGINS WITHIN

The tongue is a force to be reckoned with. We can both curse and bless with it. What an interesting instrument. We can make someone's day with it or we can wreck someone's day with it, all in the same day.

Some are very skilled with their tongue while others seem to be oblivious to its power. God says death and life are in the power of the tongue. With it, we bless God and curse man who has been made in the similitude of God. This ought not to be so; bitter water and sweet both flowing out of the same fountain.

We've all experienced the effects of someone speaking harshly to us or using words to even bring us to tears while on the other hand we've also experienced words of love and kindness that have either comforted us in times of brokenness or brought us tears of joy.

I've worked as a personal assistant for the comedian Michael Jr. This afforded me the opportunity to see the work and effort that go into bringing joy and laughter into the lives of others. I've worked in a conglomerate of industries; this was by far the most intriguing. In this, I saw the power of words staged to bring life and strength to others through joy and laughter.

> As a side note, Michael did a documentary on DVD called "Comedy: The Road Less Traveled". It's a comedy tour like no other. Michael Jr. offers his gift of comedy to the homeless on Skid Row in Los Angeles, abused children in Colorado, imprisoned youth in California, and those suffering from HIV in Fort Worth, Texas. It brings you face to face and heart to heart with hurting souls across America. This DVD motivates people to do something more, to step out of their comfort zone and make a difference by showing a way to give tangible love to the forgotten and outcast. Amazing person, amazing documentary. - www.michaeljr.com)

What is the phenomenon with the power of our words? It comes from being made in His image and after His likeness. God said, "Light be," and light was and light has never ceased to exist.

Our words are tangible, recordable things. The power that's released in them comes from within. Jesus said, "Out of the abundance of the heart the mouth speaks." He also said, in Matthew 12:35-37, "A good man out of the good treasure of his heart brings good things, and an evil man out of the evil treasure brings forth evil things. But I say to you that for every idle word men may speak, they will give an account of it in the day of judgment. For by your words you will be justified, and by your words, you will be condemned."

POWER AT ITS CORE

The words of our mouths release the substance, attitude, and position of the heart. The heart is a very powerful thing that God has given us. It carries emotions and thoughts. As a man thinks in his heart so is he.

The perception that is created from the compilation of the thoughts and emotions of the heart is conveyed or communicated through the words of our mouths.

The perception of heart is very important. We are to pay close attention to "how" we hear because how we hear is crucial to what we get out of what we're hearing. It is how we hear that builds heart perception.

For instance, a joyful person who believes in looking for the best in everything can listen to some very upsetting news and they will seek to find the good or redemption in the situation. On the other hand, a negative, angry, critical person will hear the same equally upsetting news and begin to use their mouths to validate their point of pessimism. They've both heard the same thing but they've both perceived differently.

Where is the pessimism coming from? It's coming from the established points of the heart that have prejudged life and concluded that there's no good to be found in anything, and see this as case-and-point to prove it. It only takes one traumatic situation to change someone's perspective. If we're not watchful of our hearts this can affect our perspective for the rest of our lives.

Oftentimes, our own life situations and circumstances cause us to prejudge all of humanity, and then all of life is seen through the lens of our own personal hurts and pains that we've held on to. Some call it, "Just being real." Yes, this is true, it's your own reality, but no one else should have to be subject to the tainted prejudices of the unresolved hurts and pains of others.

There are a few problems with the "just being real" syndrome. One, we will draw to ourselves the condition of our own hearts so, inevitably, we will "magnetize", if-you-will, the content of our own hearts. That's a common teaching of life coaches, this is nothing new (maybe forgotten but not new). In this train of thought, one becomes surrounded by the "negativity" of life. Bah, humbug, all of life is lousy. This state of mind leaves one grappling for scraps of joy.

Secondly, it becomes cyclic. A continued cycle of confirming events causes prejudices to begin to form based on a limited survey of biased circumstances that was formed because of what the heart has magnetized unto itself. All of life's surveying data is now contaminated.

Thirdly, living an unending cycle of disheartening or even tragic things as the norm prejudices and hardens the heart. This is a dangerous place to be. When the heart becomes hard, it can't see any way out. There's no resolve and no reprieve in sight.

As a life coach for healthy living, I help my clients to understand the importance of perspective. When food is re-categorized as healthy or "unhealthy", the term "unhealthy" is perceived as "not as healthy as", in a comparison between the two, implying that there is some small percentage of "healthy" in the "unhealthy". Unhealthy is a soft term for "not so good for you, but ok to eat".

When something is "not so good for you, but ok to eat" if your "want to" is strong enough, you'll eat it. Replacing the term "unhealthy" with "detrimental" gives a very different perception. Saying that it is either healthy for you or detrimental to your health, makes it very black and white. Someone would eat something unhealthy if they really wanted it, but if it was detrimental, then that's a different story. Detrimental infers that it has the possibility of being fatal. The "want to" now loses its appetite.

Either it's healthy for you or it's not. If you're choosing to live healthily and eat healthy then anything else, no matter how you term it, apart from healthy, is out of the question for you. A stance for eating healthy has to be made, not eating healthier.

For example, my daughter and I were hungry, it was very late at night and our only options at that hour were fast food drive thru-s. Ordinarily, we would have chosen the better tasting one with what looked like real chicken out of the "unhealthy" eateries. My daughter opted for fries and I opted for nothing.

She asked why I didn't just have some fries. I told her I made a heart choice, in that moment. Since there were no healthy choices available, I had nothing to choose from. I chose to act as though there was no food to be found instead of settling for the unhealthy that was detrimental to my health and my new way of eating.

Negative thinking has to be deemed detrimental to a healthy heart. It is not working for you, it's working against you. It's in opposition to a healthy perspective. Just because negativity is available doesn't mean you have to partake of it. The same way I made fast-food obsolete by choice, anyone can render negative thinking obsolete. It's a choice. It may be difficult at first because of a bad habit, but with diligence habits can be changed.

When a health crisis arises as the fruit of bad choices, we're left grappling to regain our health, and now we want to "make healthy choices". This is true for the heart as well. Continued negative thoughts about self and others affect so many areas of our lives, as we found out from Dr. Leaf.

For a new path of good choices to be made, bad habits have to be replaced with good habits and unhealthy appetites have to change. Sometimes these things are easier to do for the body than they are for the soul. Our heart frequently makes excuses for our choices to justify what we think, how we reason or how we choose to behave. Excuses are reasons to remain.

No one else is responsible for the health, condition and atmosphere of my heart but me. Only I am responsible for what goes in. I have to guard my ear gates and eye gates. These are the points of entry for the heart. Appetite is the triggering mechanism of the heart that has to be closely monitored. The appetite is regulated by its feeding schedule. What you want to decrease, starve the appetite. What you want to increase, feed the appetite for it.

The heart is the very core and center of our lives. If it is hurt, wounded, broken or offended, it affects our daily living; if it's filled with vitality, joy and thanksgiving, it affects our daily living. Every issue of our lives springs forth from the very core of our being, the heart.

POWER LIVING

A heart that hates evil, pride, arrogance, the evil way and the perverse mouth, and that embraces humility will live a life of riches and honor. The love and hate emotions and attitudes of the heart are powerful forces. There are things we are to hate, as there are things we are to love, and we're not to get them twisted.

Hate repels and love draws and builds. When used purposefully and appropriately, they construct and fortify powerful living. They are the hidden root source of power words that flow from our hearts.

When a heart is filled with hate, it spews forth words of fury; when a heart is filled with love, words of life, love, and vitality flow from the heart. The force of emotions in our words can be compared to water from a fire hydrant hose, which differs greatly from an old-fashioned backyard water hose.

Hearts that are abundantly filled with love can propel a life of power and freedom for not only self but others as well. Hatred, pride, arrogance, an evil way and perverse mouth and thinking opposes a healthy heart.

I remember when God taught me this great, life-changing secret. I had made some really, really, really bad choices, some that I thought I'd never, ever do. When I talked to God about it, I told Him He had to help me because I was afraid of myself. I don't know what I would or wouldn't do.

He showed me that I didn't hate what I was doing. Honestly speaking, I didn't. He pointed out that I actually enjoyed what I was doing but I hated that "it" was "wrong" because I didn't want to be doing anything wrong. I wanted it to be alright so that I didn't feel guilty about it.

Isn't that our natural response to the pleasures of sin? Somebody agree with me that it's okay so that I don't feel guilty about doing what I already know is wrong; somebody make the wrong of it go away.

I wasn't hating what I was doing, I was hating that it was wrong because "I wanted to be right" in doing what I was doing, having my own way—that's called getting it twisted!

When God speaks to us, it's ALWAYS in love and power to set free. It may not feel like it at first but give it a moment; when the love radiates through its power shatters the bondage. A light will come on, and you will wonder how you ever became entangled in darkness like that.

His love, light and freedom make you feel like a whole different person. The experience will make you wonder who that other person was who was trying to live life inside of you.

I wanted Him to pry me loose of the bondage. He just stood back and said, "No, you can do it." Bondage makes you feel powerless because of the darkness that has shrouded the heart. It blinds the mind and obscures perspective. But, again, He knows what He's placed on the inside of us that is just waiting to be revealed.

He just changed my perspective of the whole thing and made liberty very simplistic. He corrected my hatred. He showed me what I was enjoying so much was actually out to kill me; it was a hidden poison. I hated being wrong (pride) when, all the time, I should have been hating the evil way. He changed my perspective of sin; it's not just wrong or incorrect, it's deadly.

I use to think sin is the wrong choice, obedience is the right choice (correct); in actuality, sin is the death choice and obedience is the life choice. That one perspective shift has not only changed my life, it has saved my life. It's like a fresh, new pair of glasses. I was able to immediately let go of those horrid "want-tos" and walk away.

Now I had some appetites and habits to change, but the bondage was gone and I just had to strengthen my appetite in humility, grace, and love, which changed those horrid appetites quite quickly.

For clarity's sake, I'll give you a simple explanation of how something can be dead and we don't even recognize it. I love fresh flowers throughout my house. Sometimes I'm a bit slow in throwing them out because I want to squeeze every bit of beauty left in them. I'll be picking off the dead petals for days.

When they're practically gone, I may occasionally hang them upside down to dry if I really want to keep them for a while longer.

One day, I was admiring the fresh flowers I had just put on the foyer table. They smelled so fresh. The colors were vibrant and beautiful. Just as clear, the Lord said to me, "You know those are dead, don't you?" Well, of course, I knew they were dead. What He was doing was pointing out something I intellectually knew but, in actuality, it was not registering true because I was unconsciously thinking they weren't yet dead, they hadn't begun to fall apart all over my table.

Even though I knew the flowers were dead from the moment they were cut from the garden, they were not registered as dead in my mind; they were still alive until I saw their decay on the table and had to clean up the mess they would soon make.

The moment the flowers were cut from the garden they were cut off from their source of life. Giving them fresh water was just prolonging the inevitable. Death had begun the moment they were cut off from their source of life.

God says, "I have placed before you death and life, choose life that you and your seed may live." He's not hiding anything from us, yet out of His love for us, He's allowing us to choose for ourselves.

The pleasure of sin has a way of falsifying the inevitable; unless it's interrupted, it always ends in death. There is a multitude of religious beliefs in the world, but none has paid for sin in our lives but Jesus. His whole life here on Earth was to walk out what it is to live a life connected to the source of life Himself, God the Father, and pay for the sin of all of mankind that has separated us from the source of life Himself.

The only people who had a problem with Jesus were the ones who wanted to have their own way and remain in their sin—and He let them.

There was a rich, young ruler who came to Him asking what he must do to be saved. Jesus said, "Sell what you have, give to the poor and come follow me." The Bible says that the guy went away sad because he had great riches.

Jesus has a way of showing you yourself. When He does, we are without excuse. It's His heart that we are not eternally separated from Him and the Father but He's not going to make anyone do anything.

Jesus did not go running after the guy and try to work things out. I don't know the guy, but my thought is that he went away sad because Jesus touched something that was close to his heart that he did not want to let go of.

God the Father said He will not have any other gods before Him. Selling everything that you have and giving to the poor is not the law of salvation. Jesus was showing him himself. In that moment, the rich young ruler chose the things that he had over the salvation that he had sought out.

Jesus is saying what He has for us is better than what we're trying to hold on to, no matter what it is. He will make Himself clear but He will not make us do anything. He showed me the way of freedom, but He was not going to make me take it and I had to put forth the effort to be free. The Bible tells us to draw near to God and He'll draw near to us.

His power in us increases as we let the lesser die that His greater can live. Just before my husband and I got married, we went to a dinner club one evening to see a friend who was singing. We used to drink socially, like have a glass or two when we were out with friends, but we didn't stock our home refrigerator or cabinets with it.

Just that day, the Lord had told me to stop social drinking. I told David and him, being from New Orleans, wasn't sure that he was down with that program since that was part of their culture. It was ok; I didn't mind if he didn't, I just wasn't going to be drinking anymore.

That evening, at dinner, for the first time ever, someone sent an unopened bottle of wine over to our table because they were leaving and were not going to have it. Well, I could have started my non-drinking program the next day but I recognized the moment and refused the wine, thanking them for it and saying, "We don't drink." [Note - recognizing those power moments is important]

After dinner, we moved over to seats directly in front of the stage to watch our friend sing. We sat next to another guest who he had invited. That other guest began to squirm in her seat. I asked her what the problem was. She said her back hurt. I asked her if I could pray for her; she said yes.

As I was praying for her I remembered that sometimes the back can be in pain when one leg is longer than the other, something that most people who have that problem are unaware of. I explained that to her and asked if I could check her feet to see if one leg was longer than the other. She allowed us to do that. (Mind you, all of this was going on right up front, just before our mutual friend went on stage).

When we prayed for her leg to grow out, which was between 1-2 inches shorter than the other, it grew right out, right there in front of her eyes! She was in shock! She said she felt it grow out! I was clapping and all excited. We finished praying for her and she accepted Jesus in her heart.

That was so exciting for me. I've prayed and have seen that same miracle multiple times now, but that was the first. That simple act of obedience before I met her opened up the door for others to receive the same miracle she received that night.

Now, mind you, none of that would have happened that night had I chosen to delay my obedience to the next day. (Delayed obedience is still disobedience; that's obedience on your terms). A whole other course of action would have been put in motion. I don't know that I would have asked her if I could pray for the pain in her back, let alone pray for her leg to grow out. I would have been in a very different place. That one single act of disobedience would have redirected the course of my evening because obedience steers one course of action and disobedience another. Whatever the justification for disobedience is, that is what becomes empowered because that now becomes the cause of action. You are a slave to whom you obey.

Now this is not a theological book on the Bible or anything like that, I'm just sharing the experiences of my life that I think will help others in their walk. They're true, they happened, so they're beyond dispute because they've already happened.

Obedience in the small things is the power gateway for the big things. Oftentimes, we want to disobey in the small things and save our obedience for the big things.

When I learned obedience in the small things, it was very surprising to see just how disobedient we can be just out of habit. The big ones are obvious, but it's the small ones that can easily go undetected if we're not watchful and it will affect our walk in the fullness of what we've been created to do and be.

He never asks us to do something we can't do; it always has to do with our "want to". It's called humility and submission.

As I said, His light and His love will show you, you. Disobedience obscures and casts a shadow of darkness, making it difficult to see when we're in disobedience.

There was no big, booming voice from heaven saying, "Don't drink anymore." It was a simple, still, small voice that could very easily have been ignored. I knew it was His voice so I've tried to learn to obey quickly. My motto is, "Don't even think about it, just do it." If I'm not obeying quickly, I get concerned because I'm obeying my own want tos, which is a big concern all by itself—we'll save that for the sequel.

Power and strength are in who He has made us to be, not in who we want to be. He is always showing us ourselves so that we can walk in the fullness of what He's created us to be. Having the components of power apart from who you are to carry and administer that power is futile.

Before any condemnation begins to speak to you, God is extremely patient and it is His heart's desire that we all live a fruitful life. It is He Who is for us and not against us. It is God Who has remained in our corner when no one else did or would. He's compassionate, kind and full of tender mercies. His mercies are new every morning. His grace and mercy are available to us daily to cover us from the repercussions of the mistakes that we make.

He has said, "Come boldly to the throne of grace and obtain mercy and find grace to help in time of need." He has freely opened up His throne to us. He is always cheering us on. His plans for us are for good and not for evil.

That is God's heart toward us and for us. That is what He has spoken and what He has written; none can change it. Though His love for us is grand and beyond compare, He also wants us to be aware of the true power and strength that we carry, and the weight of its responsibility. Much is required of whomsoever is given much. With responsibility comes reward and/or consequences.

We are created from the Creator of heaven and Earth, in His Image and after His Likeness. Heaven is His throne and the earth is His footstool. Our responsibility is great but we come from great stock.

The meditation of our hearts is essential to a healthy heart and a healthy self-image. Meditation is simply the inner conversation of the heart. The content of our heart is contingent upon what goes in through our ear gates and eye gates.

As I said earlier in chapter five, we are to diligently guard our hearts because out of it flow the issues of our lives. Our life issues are steered by the power of our tongue.

These four things—fear of the Lord, humility, love and forgiveness—are border boundaries that protect the heart and keep the issues of life flowing from our hearts for healthy living and into the lives of others to perpetuate healthy community.

8 ARMED FORCES

RELATIONSHIP RELATIONSHIP RELATIONSHIP

At this point, you can see that it is optimal that we know and operate in who we are designed to be. The thought that so many of us have had at one time or another, "I know there is so much more to me." is true. There is a wealth untapped potential in all of us. It's in our relationships with others, but more importantly our relationship with our creator that uncovers the treasures of gold within.

I've been taught quite a bit about Christianity and faith. There was a time when I was really trying very hard to walk out what I had been taught, being diligent to dot every "i" and cross every "t". It just didn't seem to be working for me, like it "seemed to be" for others.

During that time, I asked God why He made this faith thing so hard. OMG... He most definitely answered me in love but it sure hurt like heck! His response was, "Why do you want to do this without Me?" It still hurts to think about, but I'm sharing this story for you to know that sometimes we can get so wrapped up in the science of Christianity (not Christian Science) and, inadvertently, exclude Christ Himself. I was trying to work out all of my faith rules and tools apart from Him; everything I learned about what He wanted for me, but it was all separate from Him.

He wants us to know that He's in everything with us, and as much or as little as we want Him to be. He knew that I didn't realize what I was doing, yet I was doing it all the same. It hurt when He said that because it was never my heart's intention to "get the goods", so-to-speak, apart from Him. It stopped me in my tracks. I was so puzzled. How was I walking by faith without Him? Well, I wasn't actually. What I was doing was considering Him a factor in the equation, when there should never have been an equation to begin with. It's about being so connected with Him in relationship that everything flows out of that place.

WHAT WE HAVE IN HIM

There are so many treasures in Him that have been hidden for us, not from us. We don't have to think or operate separately from Him. An orphaned heart does not know or perceive the Father's love. It is a foreign concept, it does not recognize how that kind of love could exist for one's self. The orphaned heart was groomed to provide for and protect self.

Rejection is at the root of an orphaned heart. People are created to receive love and in particular, the love of a father. Studies have shown that the love of a mother and the love of a father are two very different types of love, and both are necessary for a healthy upbringing. I'm not saying if you don't have both you're not emotionally healthy.

What I am saying is we were designed to work and grow at our optimal level with the love of both parents. Of course, there are single parents who do amazing jobs as single parents.

There are also families that have both the mother and the father whose households aren't as healthy as some single parent households because one or both parents are absentee parents. In some cases, either one or both parents were not properly nurtured in God's love to be able to love their children appropriately. This is not about the exception to the rule but about how it was designed to work optimally.

There's a lady named Cheryl Salem who has taught on what the absence of mother does to a child and what the absence of a father does to a child. Because it takes the two to create the child, for the sake of wholeness, it requires the components of love from the both that created the child to feel wholly loved.

When our perspective is right, things begin to fall into place. My perspective was off. I should have been seeing Him through relationship, not as a factor in what I wanted from the relationship. He weighs the thoughts and intents of the heart. That is where none shall escape. If our hearts are to truly know Him, He'll remove all of the dross that contaminates the purity of our hearts. Is that what we really want, a relationship with Papa God Who we can truly be vulnerable and transparent with, free from retribution because His grace has been freely given to us?

He said when a man's ways please Him, He'd make even our enemies at peace with us. When our identity is intact, as sons and daughters of the Most High God, His love and protection act as armed forces on our behalf. He not only provides for us but He protects us. Someone who abides in sonship does not quibble over protection; it's a given.

Sonship carries birthrights from being born of His Spirit. If our souls are tarnished from the effects of being an orphan, then we'll always feel the need to protect ourselves and erect various walls of protection and construct plans of war.

SONSHIP IS SIMPLE

Entering into sonship is simple. God already took the first step when Jesus paid for the sin of humanity and victory was sealed when He was raised from the dead. All we have to do is say yes to what was already taken care of on our behalf.

When I offer a free product on my website, although it's available to all, the only ones who receive it are those who say yes to the offer. Jesus has paid the price for restored sonship back to the Father but you have to accept the offer that is freely given. Romans 10:9-10 says if you believe in your heart and confess with your mouth, you'll be saved.

When I was in my late twenties, my family and I had one of our large family reunions. We were picking up family members all over the state and driving and caravanning to another state for the reunion. Every so often, passengers would swap cars when we made our periodic pit stops.

On one of the stops, the Lord wanted me to ride in the car with one of my uncles who was riding by himself. This one particular uncle was a trucker and was in a motorcycle gang. My husband use to say I have a very "colorful" family. I LOVE my colorful family. They're so much fun. One family member was even in the circus! I loved my uncle dearly but I did not want to ride with him. He smoked profusely! All I could think of was my hair smelling like smoke when we got there, plus I wouldn't be able to handle all of that smoke for three to four hours nonstop.

The Lord reminded me of when I used to smoke... Well, that took care of that conversation. He wanted me to pray with him a prayer of salvation. Well, I always talked to my uncle when he'd come to the house and ask him if he wanted to pray with me and he'd always say, "Next time."

If God tells you to do something, He knows when someone's heart is ready. He told me exactly what to say to him. It was very simple. I just asked him did he believe that Jesus did what He did for him. He said yes he did. I told him he didn't have to do anything but tell God, thank you and receive it, bam! Done. All he said was, "God, I believe that Jesus died on the cross for my sin and paid the price for everything I've ever done. I ask you to forgive me and I receive the price that He paid for my life. I ask you to be Lord of my life. In Jesus' Name, Amen." That's the simplicity of the gospel. That's the simplicity of being restored to son-ship with God.

Religion tries to make people earn what Jesus already paid for. God knew we couldn't earn it so He paid for it for us. It's not complicated. Religion wants to hold qualifiers over our heads. God says that His simplicity of the gospel confounds the wise.

God is for us. He's not against us. He wants all that He's paid for to be ours. He did not require that we have to pay for it for ourselves. He did not require that we have to qualify for protection. Sons do not earn protection. Sons do not earn an inheritance.

His angels encircle those who fear Him. There is supernatural protection that is sent to protect us when we honor Who He is in our lives. There are more that are for us than are against us. God has seriously stacked the deck in our favor.

I don't care what it looks like; He established the end from the beginning. Jesus was the lamb slain before the foundation of the earth. Who is it that begins a project and does not count the cost? Of course, God has counted the cost. Before Earth was ever inhabited by man, God already made preparation for every mistake we could ever make. In His infinite wisdom, He made provision for those who are called by His name and who fear

Him. There is a winning side because He created it. No one is subject to loss in Him. He has armed forces to take care of us and fight for us.

You can say the same prayer that my uncle did. Just repeat what he said for your self. Choose to believe it with your heart when you say the prayer and receive restored son-ship for yourself. If you do happen to pray this prayer, I'd love to hear from you and give you my meditation CD for free. Just go to my website, www.lifeinHim.us and put the code NewLifeinHim at the checkout and you will get the MP3 download for free.

Life in Him is grand! He didn't say it would be easy but He did say He would not leave us as orphans and He would give us His joy. It has definitely been an adventure like none other.

9 REAL LOVE IS NOT FOR WIMPS

GENUINE LOVE

Picking back up from chapter four where I was sharing some love experiences that I've had, in this chapter, I want to share with you about His love in us that is not for the faint of heart. His love requires character muscles. In chapter four you saw how love is a choice when you know that it's within you and you have access to it.

This chapter is more about having a genuine love that walks above circumstances that most would find it easier to flee from. Being fortified in the strength that His love carries empower us to live a life of power, strength and authority.

We all have our own definition of love. By default, we're taught to love by how we've been raised, which, the majority of the time, is not the same as God's perspective of love. God's love is not for wimps. It is strong and powerful, yet gentle and inviting. The genuineness of God's love never fails. His love is not for the faint of heart because His love requires us to love apart from ourselves.

Most want to love inclusive of self, as in loving someone because of what can be gained from showing them love. God's love is because of Who He is. He loved us when we were at our worst. He loved us when we didn't love ourselves. We are able to love Him and others because He first loved us.

His love is obtainable. Jesus said we are to love one another as He's loved us. When we love because of who we are or who we're becoming in Him, and not because of what we can get out of it, we're making choices that empower His love, strength and authority to flow through us.

His love only comes out of a relationship with Him and it cannot be faked, forged or fabricated. I heard someone once say, "Fake it till you make it." Hmmm, I get what they're alluding to, but, in actuality, by faking it till you make it, you're just fooling yourself, because in your heart you're creating a pattern of deception. You know you're faking it and the more you do it, the easier it becomes and the easier it becomes the more likely you are to do it more often, creating within yourself a habit of falsehood.

God's love is genuine. We deserve genuine love. We should pursue His love so that we can give genuine love to others.

I asked the Lord to show me how to genuinely love people from my heart, whether they knew it or not. I could do the "Christian thing" and "pretend to love" them but God knows the thoughts and intents of my heart. That was not going to fly very far with Him. I wanted a love that came from His heart, through me to them. This would be a love that He was surely pleased with.

If I waited for myself to grow in love for people, it may or may not happen. Mankind has a tendency to love what's like unto himself. I had to be real with me. There were people who really got on my last nerve. I was not going to put the blame on it being a bad day. No, I just did not like that person and I didn't want to try to either. Well, that's really lovely. Wasn't that real "Christian" of me.

There's no sense in pretending to love someone when you really don't. It only truly matters to God and you can't fool God, He already knows what's in your heart. I was just honest with God and I was expecting an honest answer back. It was simple and not very complicated. When my heart is stirred with His heart, it's very easy to love those I really like and those who I really don't care for. I can love them both alike because His love stirred up in me helps me to see them the way He sees them.

As in chapter four, you can draw from the well of love within you by choice, when you know how to stir that love up on the inside. To walk in the strength and power that it provides, His love in us has to become who we are and what we identify with, not something that we do to please God or man.

When we walk in God's love as a way of life and it's no longer a struggle, it comes with strength and authority. The choice that empowers the flow of this authority in our lives is a surrendered life of love.

ATTITUDE AFFECTS EVERYTHING

The word surrender can be apprehensive to some. It has a connotation of weakness when in actuality it is indicative of strength. Jesus surrendered His life when He laid it down. He said no man takes His life. He had the power (authority) to lay it down and the power (authority) to take it up again.

Attitude is defined by Google as "a settled way of thinking or feeling about someone or something, typically one that is reflected in a person's behavior."

What I find interesting about that particular definition of the word attitude is the word "settled". That's conclusive to me. I like to think of the word attitude as the heart's reflection of its position towards what it believes. Your attitude has a posture towards what you believe; it takes a position, a stance, it is not neutral, per se.

When we make a heart stance of I love, regardless of anything else, this is who I am and this is what I do, we've set ourselves in a position of power and strength. We have the ability to set our hearts in an attitude of love and call it settled. If we don't, it's too easy to waver back and forth emotionally because of reasonings. There's no strength in wavering. A wavering heart cannot be trusted.

Choosing love ahead of the game fortifies our strength against anger, bitterness, evil thinking, strife, contention and malice. These are all emotional traps that drain life and strength out of you. Then, out of self-preservation, a falsified persona of protection immerges, the "_itchy" attitude.

Governing the internal posture of your mind is of the utmost importance. You can't reign over what you give place to. Jesus said, in John 14:30 AMP, "the prince (evil genius, ruler) of the world is coming. And he has no claim on Me. [He has nothing in common with Me; there is nothing in Me that belongs to him, and he has no power over Me.]"

I love John 14:30 in the Amplified Bible because it speaks very plainly. "[He has nothing in common with Me; there is nothing in Me that belongs to him, and he has no power over Me.]" The enemy's power over anyone is in direct relation to what is in them that belongs to him or what he has in common with them.

We are told to give the devil no place. That word place is topos in Greek, where we get our word topography from. We are not to give him a topographical grain of sand. When we maintain an attitude of love, the devil has no place.

Love is kind and patient, it's not puffed up, nor is it self-seeking, it thinks no evil. A love stance has to begin in our thoughts and the meditations of our hearts. In making a stance for love, we'll become more aware of the thoughts in our hearts that will give place to love, self-seeking or evil.

There is one person I know who has done some very evil and self-seeking things to me and my family. She was very challenging to my love walk. Some of the malicious things she would do were just outrageous and startling.

Early on, I saw things that lent themselves to her having the capability of doing what she's done. Before she could possibly swing my way, I made a stance in my heart that neither she nor her antics would move me out of the love of God.

Oftentimes, I would forgive her right there in the moment and pray for her. God gave me compassion for her to see how much she must really hurt inside, to find joy in causing other people pain. She would do scandalously hideous things and laugh about them and try to pull others in on her laughter.

Making my love stance ahead of time saved me many an upset and gave me foresight and fortitude to win on every front. Love never fails. It first and foremost protects our heart, from whence the issues of our lives flow.

Secondly, it flavors our life with peace, joy, goodness and self-control to rule within and govern our actions. We are no longer subject to the wiles of others or the whims of life.

We fortify our hearts in genuine love when the enemy comes against us, he has nothing in common with us that gives him power over us.

The culture of our Kingdom is love. We can identify with the Kingdom of God, not only because He's restored us back to right relationship with Him but also because He's given us the free choice to live as He does, in life, love and freedom.

10 QUEENS REIGN

LIFE IN HIM

Sometimes I'll close my eyes and see how deep I can press into God's heart. I fix my mind on how kind and loving He is. I like to take the time to feel and experience His goodness in my heart.

The Bible says to be still and know that He is God. It's a great thing to be able to stop in moments of our day to turn inward and acknowledge His Presence and His father's heart for us. Sometimes I squeeze my eyes shut like a little girl and just say, "I love you bunches and bunches, a whole lot, and I welcome Your love for me." We have to welcome His love into our hearts.

Acts 17:28 says it is in Him that we move and live and have our being. All of who we are created to be is in Him. He reigns as King of kings and Lord of lords. He is all supreme. Our identity in Him is that we reign as He reigns. He has made it all possible, the choice is ours.

When we take the time to be as little children in His arms, it relinquishes to Him our own necessity to be in control. For me, it's my way of telling Him, "I trust You and I'm thankful I do not have to do life alone."

We are not to be subservient to the circumstances of life, but to reign in His victory that conquered death, hell, and the grave. To conquer death, hell and the grave, pretty much sums up the worst of any situation.

There is nothing Jesus can't handle on our behalf. Being born of His Spirit makes us heirs of His Kingdom. Being heirs of the Kingdom of God, we have a Kingdom that backs us. His grace is more than enough. There is no need to fight for ourselves. He's our rock and our defense.

We all operate from the kingdom that we identify with. It is imperative we know the kingdom we're born of, if we don't, we'll remain subservient to a lesser kingdom and carry the characteristics of that kingdom.

I'm from North Carolina, located in the southeastern part of the United States of America. It's known for the beauty of country living. My dad always used to say, "You can take the girl out of the country, but you can't take the country out of the girl."

The same holds true concerning what kingdom we identify with. When we're truly born of His Spirit and identify with who we are in Him, although we may be in a different geographical location, we should be inseparable from the culture of our kingdom.

Another example is the mom of a friend of mine. They're from Guatemala. Guatemalans celebrate Mother's Day on a different day than we do here in America. Her mom so identifies with the culture of her country that she still only recognizes the official Guatemalan Mother's Day. To her, American Mother's Day is not the "real" Mother's Day.

There's a culture in the Kingdom of God. It's love, joy, and peace. To choose love, to choose joy, to choose peace, we have to let go of everything that is the polar opposite of love, joy and peace. His grace enables us to walk unencumbered in His love, joy and peace. Grace gives us what I call tangle-free love, tangle-free joy, and tangle-free peace. We can choose on purpose to make these three things our reality.

God makes some very interesting statements in the Bible. Psalm 8:5 (AMP) says something very powerful. It says we are made a little lower than Elohim; God (it's translated angels but the original Hebrew is Elohim). Exodus 7:1 says God said to Moses that He made him as God to Pharaoh to declare His will and purpose to him. Psalm 8:6 says, "You have made him (man) to have dominion over the works of Your hands; You have put all things under his feet."

God not only chooses to have us as His representatives in the earth, but we're representatives from His monarchy. When this truth becomes real on the inside of us, there's a dominion and authority that we'll naturally walk in. Confidence comes with knowing who we are. There's a rest and peace in that place. No more striving to be, because we know who we are.

Living in Los Angeles, California, one of the "it" and "cool" cities, I certainly didn't feel like I "fit in". Growing in my relationship with the Lord brought freedom because of His love for me. He loved me so much and so unconditionally that I grew in confidence and began to enjoy being myself. I was simply loved fiercely and unconditionally; God Himself loved me. Finding rest in His love allows His Kingdom to flow freely from us, for others to taste and see that He is good.

SPEAK SOFTLY AND CARRY A BIG STICK

President Theodore Roosevelt is quoted as saying, "Speak softly and carry a big stick; you will go far." That's similar to another quote that I've heard along the way, "Meekness is strength under control."

In walking with God, I began to walk in an authority that I was unaware of. I found the confidence that comes from the purity of His love; it yields an authority that comes innately. Yes, we have authority because of the Name of Jesus, but to carry that authority from within because of whose we are is very different. I would liken it to President Roosevelt's quote, "Speak softly and carry a big stick..."

My close friends used to tell me that I intimidated people. I found that puzzling and somewhat disturbing because once His confidence had drawn me out of my shell, I really liked people and loved getting to know them.

Then a very close friend pointed out to me that it was the authority that I walked in that was intimidating to some. Well, I surely wasn't trying to intimidate anyone or "exert" or "walk in authority", I just wanted to love God, love people and enjoy life.

I was well aware of the authority that I carried because of knowing and being confident in whose I am. His love is so beautiful that I want everyone to know about it. His love empowers and draws out our true identity, which carries His authority, because of whose we are. When we press full force into His love, His authority is a part of the package deal. It's His authority that releases you to be all that you were created to be.

Unbeknownst to myself, I was walking in His authority without trying, yet when I needed it, it was there—and all because of the empowerment of His love. It's like Dad giving you that stamp of approval to go out full of confidence and strength because He's backing you. I remember oftentimes thinking, if God said yes I could, all noes were irrelevant. The opposition didn't matter; God said yes.

When we know who we are, confident in who we are, and comfortable in our own skin, there's an authority that we carry to speak to and address any given situation. Humility is what confidence from God looks like. His love and His authority yield humility. It's that quiet strength, whose weight is made up of love that authorizes us to do what is necessary for any given situation.

LET FREEDOM REIGN

There's a blog post that I would like to share with you. It is one inspiring stance of love, honesty and transparency. I don't personally know this person, only through having mutual friends on Instagram. However, I was given permission to include the blog, in its entirety, for the sake of keeping it in its proper context.

It's quite empowering because it typifies the epitome of a queen reigning in love and humility. People and circumstances can be challenging at times. How do we remain in a place of rest in His love, but have an answer to life's tough situations?

The crux of this book is there is always a way to say what you need to say while maintaining the love, style and grace with which you were born. Esther Houston does a marvelous job of this in her post! Enjoy.

It Is For Freedom

That We Have Been Set Free

Esther Houston

I get a lot of backlash for doing what I do. I think that comes as no surprise to most of you. How can I like clothes and work in fashion while being in a family of well-known pastors? Travesty! That is just highly inappropriate. You can't try to look good and love Jesus. You can't like clothes, that's just vain! No way! It's ludicrous! Just awful.

Well, I don't believe that is true. So since I have been accused of my "message" being unclear, I thought I'd clear that up so that nobody will have to go about their lives being 'confused' by mine. (Haha. Isn't that funny how we blame people for our own confusion... For goodness sakes, be secure in what you believe! Where is our personal conviction?!)

Let's go back a few years, when I first came into what I knew was a relationship with God. Reminisce... I love those moments when you bring yourself back to where you were and just remember... It's never good to forget where you come from. My friend Carl Lentz says, "Let's not forget that we WERE the woman at the well before we started to judge women at the well..." (Just saying).

**Let's not forget that we WERE the woman at the
well before we started to judge women at the well.**

One of the first things I experienced about God was a
feeling of freedom. Everybody is always talking about
rules that come with religion. My experience was the
very opposite. For the first time, I realized that I no
longer had to prove myself on a daily basis because I
had ALREADY been accepted. I was already loved... I
didn't have to win anybody's love... Didn't have to prove
that I was good enough. That's why Jesus came—to
take the pressure off me and pay the price for me... So
that we could "cast all our cares upon Him and lay ALL
of our burdens at His feet."

However, that just seems too good to be true.
Nothing in life is free, nothing in life is easy, right? But
our salvation seems to be; we have been accepted, yet
not because of our works. By faith, we have been saved.
What a revelation! We can now live FROM a place of
acceptance, not FOR acceptance. Wow. Groundbreaking.

**We can now live FROM a place of acceptance, not
FOR acceptance.**

Now a little background. You have to understand
how I lived most of my life. I never felt secure, never felt
free. I always had to prove myself and make known the
reasons why I was worthy of my position and status. Do
you understand how exhausting that is? Always putting
on masks. Always putting a smile on your face while you
silently and slowly break down. Always keeping up a

thousand relationships when you actually have none. When I felt God's presence, what changed me was an instant sense of acceptance and love. I no longer had to prove myself. What a crazy concept. I was already accepted. Now I can exhale. Years and years of insecurity.

Not the kind of insecurity you could ever tell, though. No way. I was very calculating. My insecurity was the type that you could NEVER tell. I was the most insecure person in the room even though I looked like I had it all figured out. Oh my gosh, maintaining those perceptions... I'm exhausted thinking about it. What would happen if anybody ever found out that I wasn't invincible? If anybody ever found out how lonely I actually was? How much I cried behind closed doors? I had anxiety just thinking about it. Take a pill. Numb it. Get over it. Move on. Be strong. Pretend. Oh, you have NO IDEA.

With Jesus also came my freedom. All the things I had to prove, all the perceptions I had to maintain—I was now free because He loves me. I was free because His love is tangible, powerful, real, sufficient and life changing. I wasn't alone anymore. I could live FROM a place of acceptance, not FOR it. Not to achieve it. Not to conquer it. But to just humbly live in a constant state of gratitude and awe. And what a difference it made.

I don't know what some Christians have been doing with their lives, but I tell you this—my relationship with Jesus is nothing but freeing. I can now breathe. I can now love. I can now pour out what has been poured into my soul. So when it comes to petty things in life like fashion and vanity and being "too sexy" and too this and too that... Listen. I am free.

Nothing can imprison me. I am saved by grace. I am loved just because. I am accepted because the price has already been paid. Now I get to live. I get to enjoy the same things that I've always had but haven't been able to find joy in because of the constant run on the treadmill. Getting so tired and yet going nowhere. Trying to catch the wind. What a waste.

However, against ALL ODDS, I married into a "big" Christian family. So now people have been trying to put me back into the same box from which I JUST CAME OUT OF. Hah. And we call ourselves Christians. Let's throw stones at the same person we were a couple of years ago. Let's tell them what to do, what's acceptable to God, how to live, what they're doing wrong, how they're not setting good examples. I'm just so confusing! I'm a pastor's wife that should know better... Should be clearer about my message... No, no, no. I'll tell you what I am: I was blind and now I can see. That's who I am.

But ok. Let me be clear about my apparent message. I prefer to take criticism rather than to pretend like I'm ok with this idea that I or anyone else should have to fit a certain mold in order to please God. What a joke. Are you kidding me?! Do you think God goes through all the trouble to reveal Himself to us personally and to offer us abundant life in Him just to then realize that we're not good enough? Can you picture our God, creator of all things, omnipotent, omniscient, thinking, "Wow. I really messed up. I thought Esther would come through. I'm quite disappointed at her performance... I should have picked somebody else... Somebody who wasn't in the fashion industry... Somebody who dressed a little more

'conservatively', who acted more like a pastor's wife..."
What does that even mean, to look like a pastor's wife?
Who made these rules anyway? I don't remember
having that as a requirement when I got married. All I
remember is being accepted and loved as I was.

God can use me. High heels and all.

According to me, that's the whole point! The point
is that I am not good enough, and neither are you by
the way. We AREN'T good enough. But God doesn't use
people who are qualified, He uses people whose hearts
cry out for change, mercy and grace. People who are
constantly on their knees asking Him to show them the
way. To enable them, to give them wisdom. And I can
tell you I am that person. So, therefore, God can use
me. High heels and all. Believe it or not. Maybe He even
purposely picked me so that I could stir things up a bit-
who knows? I don't know. What I DO know is that He
picked me. And He also picked you.

**I HAVE BEEN SET FREE. What I do no longer
defines me.**

I HAVE BEEN SET FREE. What I do no longer defines
me. Who I am is no longer a mask. How I live no longer
dictates my status. God has loved me, saved me AND
has set me free. Although I respect all of your opinions,
it doesn't really matter. I'm the daughter of the King.
I'm a princess. I'm God's favorite. I'm His chosen one.

He took me out of darkness and into His light. He allowed me to see Him while I was blind. He loved me when I didn't deserve it. He pursued me. He was faithful when I was not. And FROM a place of freedom, I will live my life. FROM a place of gratitude, I will live in awe. And out of my brokenness, He will use me.

He always had a plan. A perfect plan we could have never thought of ourselves. Do you think it's out of His control that I'm here? That you're here? That we're here? I think not... Be free and make a difference. Stop worrying about petty things. Fix your eyes upon Jesus. He could use fewer referees and more team players; less critics and more willingness to actually do the work...

Esther

This book has been in so many stages of refinement, rework, rewrite; I can't even begin to tell you. It led to sheer exhaustion at times. When I thought I was finally done and it was on its way for the last edit, I read Esther's post. God has absolutely perfect timing. I did not have a really fine example of what I wanted to share about what it looked like to reign as a queen in uncomfortable circumstances, but this blog post said it all, and to top it off, her name is Esther (as in Queen Esther) :)

I read her post over and over again. It brings me to tears because I truly hear the heart's cry of many, just like Esther's; of those who have been injured by others and did not know how to address it or respond, so they remained silent and also of those who have experienced the struggle for identity from the emptiness of life without Christ.

Keeping an attitude of humility towards others and the issues of life keep us in a place of tenderness to show love in difficult situations. Humility has no self-justification; so there is never a need for self-defense. Christ is our defense; He's our rock and our refuge. He'll bring justice wherever it's needed.

Esther is definitely not speaking from a place of self-justification, but rather a place of liberty that sets captives free. Her voice is Christ speaking for those who've experienced the same wounds, hurts, pains and emptiness, yet have not been able to speak for themselves.

I believe Esther's voice has released a sound for many captives to be set free from the muzzling silencer of religion and the leanness of soul. Please know who the Son has set free is free indeed. The door is open; step through it and walk freely.

I hope you've enjoyed reading Fight Like A Lady. If I can be of any help, please feel free to contact me through the information on my website. http://www.LifeinHim.us

www.ingramcontent.com/pod-product-compliance
Lightning Source LLC
LaVergne TN
LVHW051416080426

835508LV00022B/3104